CHICAGO
SPORTS
QUIZ

Brenda Alesii
&
Daniel Locche

A Citadel Press Book
Published by Carol Publishing Group

A Citadel Press Book
Published by Carol Publishing Group

Citadel Press is a registered trademark of Carol
Communications, Inc.

Editorial Offices: 600 Madison Avenue, New York, N.Y. 10022
Sales & Distribution Offices: 120 Enterprise Avenue, Secaucus,
    N.J. 07094
In Canada: Canadian Manda Group, P.O. Box 920, Station U,
    Toronto, Ontario M8Z 5P9

Queries regarding rights and permissions should be addressed to
Carol Publishing Group, 600 Madison Avenue, New York, N.Y. 10022

Carol Publishing Group books are available at special discounts
for bulk purchases, for sales promotions, fund-raising, or
educational purposes. Special editions can be created to specifications.
For details, contact Special Sales Department, Carol Publishing
Group, 120 Enterprise Avenue, Secaucus, N.J. 07094

Manufactured in the United States of America
10 9 8 7 6 5 4 3 2 1

Library of Congress Cataloging-in-Publication Data

Alesii, Brenda.
    Chicago sports quiz / by Brenda Alesii & Daniel Locche.
        p.   cm.
    ISBN 0-8065-1372-1
    1. Sports-Illinois-Chicago-Miscellanea.   I. Locche, Dan.
II. Title.
    GV854.5.C4A44   1992
    796'.09773'11—dc20   92-19305
                                                       CIP

Acknowledgments

Our intention in writing *Chicago Sports Quiz* was to attempt something unique in both the sports and reference formats. The plan was to examine every team in the "big four" from the club's inception to the present. Did we achieve our objectives? The ultimate judge is always the reader.

As with our previous Quiz books, it has been our privilege to research and learn about the histories, the facts and foibles, and the distinctive characteristics of each franchise and its players. We hope you find *Chicago Sports Quiz* to be the consummate sports reference tool, one that embodies the teams' joys and frustrations and their sometimes offbeat and fascinating pasts.

Writing a book of this nature is not possible without the cooperation of many, including the following:

Wayne Patterson and the Naismith Memorial Basketball Hall of Fame
Bill Deane and the Baseball Hall of Fame
Joe Horrigan and the Football Hall of Fame
Phil Pritchart and the Hockey Hall of Fame
The teams: Bears, Cubs, White Sox, Bulls, and Blackhawks

We would be remiss if we didn't thank our families and friends, who offer unending support and who tolerate us around deadline time. We also salute a man who is perceptive enough to recognize great ideas, Bob Salomon of Carol Publishing Group.

Photos contained in this book have been acquired from the following sources:

Basketball: Hall of Fame, Springfield, Massachusetts
Baseball: National Baseball Library, Cooperstown, New York
Football: Hall of Fame, Canton, Ohio, and NFL Properties
Hockey: Hall of Fame, Toronto, Ontario, Canada

How to Use
Chicago Sports Quiz

Chicago Sports Quiz is divided into five chapters: The Bears, Cubs, White Sox, Bulls, and Blackhawks. Each section contains questions, answers, and "fast facts" pertaining to the particular team.

For your convenience, the question page always precedes the answer page; questions are grouped separately from their respective answers. (A "Q" represents a question, while an "A" indicates an answer.) Each chapter reflects the chronology of the team; it is divided into separate categories in the following manner: "Suits" denotes coaches, managers, and front-office personnel; "Uniforms" involves the players; "Setting the Standard" is about records; "FYI" is general information; "Glory Days" covers the playoffs and any postseason activity; and "Trades, Waives, and Acquisitions" are just that.

The questions are current as of June 1992.

As is generally recognized, Chicago is home to some of the most knowledgeable sports fans in the country. In compiling the hundreds of questions and answers, we may have overlooked some facts and figures. We ask your indulgence.

Contents

BIBLIOGRAPHY

The Baseball Encyclopedia. New York: Macmillan, 1990.

Baylor, Don, and Claire Smith. *Don Baylor—Nothing But the Truth: A Baseball Life.* New York: St. Martin's Press, 1989.

Carter, Craig. *The Complete Baseball Record Book.* St. Louis: The Sporting News, 1991.

Charlton, James. *The Baseball Chronology.* New York: Macmillan, 1991.

Coberly, Rich. *The No-Hit Hall of Fame.* Newport Beach: Triple Play Publications, 1985.

Enright, Jim. *Baseball's Great Teams—Chicago Cubs.* New York: Macmillan, 1975.

Gallen, David. *The Baseball Chronicles.* New York: Carroll & Graf Publishers, 1991.

Hollander, Zander, and Alex Sachare, eds. *The Official NBA Basketball Encyclopedia.* New York: Villard Books, 1989.

Magnuson, Keith, and Robert Bradford. *None Against.* New York: Dodd, Mead, 1973.

Manley, Martin. *Basketball Heaven.* New York: Doubleday, 1989.

McMahon, Jim, and Bob Verdi. *McMahon.* New York: Warner Books, 1986.

Neft, David S., and Richard M. Cohen. *The Football Encyclopedia.* New York: St. Martin's Press, 1991.

Pfeiffer, Gerald L. *The Chicago Blackhawks, A Sixty Year History.* Chicago: Windy City Publishing, 1986.

Reichler, Joseph. *The Baseball Trade Register.* New York: Collier Books, 1984.

Ritter, Lawrence, and Donald Honig. *The 100 Greatest Baseball Players of All Time.* New York: Crown Publishers, 1981.

Shatzkin, Mike, ed. *The Ballplayers.* New York: Arbor House, 1990.

Sloan, Dave, and Alex Sachare. *The Sporting News' NBA Guide.* St. Louis: The Sporting News, 1991.

Thorn, John, and Peter Palmer. *Total Baseball.* New York: Warner Books, 1989.

Whittingham, Richard. *The Chicago Bears—From George Halas to Super Bowl XX.* New York: Simon & Schuster, 1987.

Chicago Bears

CHICAGO BEARS

Chicago Bears—1934 Western Champions.

THE SUITS

Q1   With what club did George Halas play professional baseball?

Q2   Halas's pro football career began with the Canton Bulldogs. What position did he play?

Q3   Halas made the NFL record books as a player on November 14, 1923. What did he do that day?

Q4   What opposing player was involved in Halas's record-setting romp?

Q5   What was the name of the pro basketball club owned by George Halas?

Q6   George Halas was named commissioner of the professional basketball league, which was in existence from 1926 to 1929. What was the name of that league?

Q7   Why did George Halas change the name of the team from the Staleys to the Bears?

Q8   After suffering through a 4–8–2 season in 1929, the Master of the Midway replaced himself as head coach. Who took over as the Bears' skipper?

Q9   Who replaced George Halas as club president while Papa Bear served in the armed forces during World War II?

Q10   While Halas served in the navy, what three men toiled as the Bears' co-coaches during the wartime era, 1943–45?

Q11   Halas turned over the reins of his team on four separate occasions. What happened when Papa Bear returned to the helm in 1933 and 1946?

CHICAGO BEARS

A1   The New York Yankees (1919: 12 games; .091 batting average going 2 for 22)

A2   Right end

A3   He returned a fumble 98 yards for a touchdown.

A4   Jim Thorpe (He had fumbled the snap for the Oorang Indians.)

A5   The Chicago Bruins (1926–29)

A6   The American Basketball League

A7   He wanted to create a relationship with the baseball Cubs in the public's mind.

A8   Ralph Jones (Over three seasons, Jones compiled a 24–10–7 record.)

A9   Ralph Brizzolara

A10   Hunk Anderson
Luke Johnsos
Paddy Driscoll
(15–11–2)

A11   The Bears won world championships on both occasions.

*** BEAR FAST FACTS ***

HALAS HIGHLIGHTS
Overall Records—480 wins, 201 losses, 35 ties (includes preseason, regular season, and postseason games)
Six NFL Championships

Q12 The Redskins wanted to hire Bear assistant coach Hunk Anderson as their head man in 1951, but George Halas would not release him from his contract unless he received a particular Washington player. Who was he?

Q13 Why did George Halas resign as the Bears coach after the 1955 season?

Q14 After a next-to-last finish in 1957, Halas returned to the head coaching position. Who was axed after only two years at the helm?

Q15 To what league position was George Halas appointed in 1970?

Q16 George Halas is one of two NFL coaches to rack up 300 or more career wins. Who is the other?

Q17 Assistant coach Luke Johnsos came up with a coaching technique in 1938 that is still used today. What did Johnsos popularize?

Q18 What Bear head coach introduced wide ends and the "men in motion" to the NFL?

Q19 Identify the Stanford coach and master football tactician who formulated the modernized T formation with George Halas.

Q20 Longtime Bear assistant coach Abe Gibron was tapped for the top job in 1971. For what four teams did the "beloved behemoth" play?

Q21 What two positions did Jim Finks play with the Pittsburgh Steelers (1949–55)?

Q22 What team was Jim Finks the vice president and general manager of before he joined the Bears in 1974?

Q23 What distinction does Jack Pardee hold in Bear coaching history?

Q24 Bear skipper Jack Pardee was being lauded as a genius after Chicago engineered a 25–21 upset over the 49ers with an all-rookie backfield. Identify the threesome who appeared in the December 7, 1975, game.

Q25 After taking the Bears from the cellar in 1975 to the playoffs in 1977, Jack Pardee unexpectedly resigned. What head coaching job did he accept immediately after leaving Chicago?

Q26 On February 16, 1978, Neill Armstrong was named head coach of the Bears. Prior to his appointment, he served as the defensive coordinator for a club familiar to Chicago. For what team was Armstrong an assistant?

CHICAGO BEARS

A12 Paul Lipscomb (Washington owner George Marshall, would not give Lipscomb up and Anderson dropped out of coaching.)

A13 He promised his wife he would retire at age 60. (Originally it was age 55, but he changed his mind when he reached that birthday.)

A14 Paddy Driscoll

A15 President of the NFC (Lamar Hunt, owner of the Chiefs, was named president of the AFC.)

A16 Don Shula

A17 He and other coaches started watching the game from the upper deck of the stadium.

A18 Ralph Jones (1930)

A19 Clark Shaughnessy

A20 Bears (1958–59)
Cleveland Browns (1950–56)
Philadelphia Eagles (1956–57)
Buffalo Bills (1949—AAFC)

A21 Defensive back
Quarterback

A22 The Minnesota Vikings

A23 Pardee was the first non-Bear to hold the job.

A24 Bob Avellini
Walter Payton
Roland Harper

A25 He joined the Washington Redskins.

A26 The Minnesota Vikings

Q27   The Bears' poor showing during the 1981 season prompted George Halas to hire an "offense consultant." Who filled the bill?

Q28   Who was hired as offensive coordinator in 1981 for the purpose of enlivening the anemic Bear attack?

Q29   Mike Ditka began his playing career with a bang as he matched a Bear record for most touchdown catches by a rookie. With what player is Ditka tied for the mark?

Q30   In what round and from what school did the Bears select Mike Ditka in the 1961 draft?

Q31   After six years in a Bear uniform, Mike Ditka was dealt to the Philadelphia Eagles. Who came to the Windy City in the 1967 trade?

Q32   What positions did Ditka coach in his nine-year career with the Dallas Cowboys?

Q33   In 1980, who broke Iron Mike's NFL record for career catches by a tight end?

Q34   Besides Mike Ditka, who are the only two men to appear in the Super Bowl as players and as head coaches?

Q35   Of the trio of coaches mentioned in the previous question, which of them scored a touchdown in the Super Bowl?

Q36   In the summer of 1988, Ditka was enshrined in the Pro Football Hall of Fame. What was unusual about his induction into the hallowed halls of Canton?

Q37   What team thrashed the Bears, 30–7, on the day Mike Ditka suffered a heart attack (November 2, 1988)?

Q38   Who served as the team's interim coach for 11 days after Ditka's heart attack?

Q39   In what hit television show did Ditka portray himself in a 1990 episode?

Q40   Name the team the Bears defeated on Monday night, September 23, 1991, marking Mike Ditka's 100th victory as an NFL head coach.

Q41   Assistant coach Greg Landry had a 17-year playing career in the NFL. What team selected the University of Massachusetts QB in the first round of the 1968 draft?

CHICAGO BEARS

A27   Jim Dooley

A28   Ted Marchibroda

A29   Harlon Hill (1954)

A30   Ditka was drafted in the first round from the University of Pittsburgh.

A31   Jack Concannon

A32   Special teams
Receivers

A33   Kellen Winslow

A34   Tom Flores (quarterback for Kansas City in Super Bowl IX and coach of
the Raiders in Super Bowls XV and XVIII)
Forest Gregg (tackle for Green Bay in Super Bowls I and II and coach of
the Bengals in Super Bowl XVI)

A35   Mike Ditka (a seven-yard pass from Roger Staubach in the Cowboys'
24–3 win over the Dolphins in Super Bowl VI)

A36   Ditka was the first tight end inducted into the Hall of Fame.

A37   The New England Patriots

A38   Vince Tobin

A39   "L.A. Law"

A40   The New York Jets (Chicago prevailed in overtime, 19–13.)

A41   The Detroit Lions

Q1   Name the Bear back who became the first pro to rush for 1,000 yards in a year.

Q2   Who was the NFL's first middle linebacker?

Q3   Who was the first player to be given the Brian Piccolo Award (the award given to the rookie who best exemplifies the courage, loyalty, teamwork, dedication, and sense of humor of the late Bear back)?

Q4   Who was the first running back to be honored with the Brian Piccolo Award?

Q5   In December 1920, sports editor Bruce Copeland of the *Rock Island Argus* put together the first all-pro team. (He called them the Big 8.) What player was selected from the Chicago club?

Q6   Why is Ed Healey a significant name in Bear history?

Q7   What nickname did Red Grange earn because of an off-season job he held?

Q8   Against what club did the Galloping Ghost make his pro debut?

Q9   Red Grange was football's first $100,000-a-year player when he signed with the Bears in 1925. What unique feature was part of his contract?

Q10   When the Bears refused Grange's demands in 1926 for one-third ownership of the team, the Ghost left to form his own team and league. What were the two organizations called?

Q11   When Red Grange caught a two-yard pass against the Portsmouth Spartans in the 1932 season, it marked the first time the Bears had won an NFL championship. Who threw the winning pass to the Galloping Ghost?

Q12   What was Red Grange's given name?

Q13   What was C. C. Pyle's relationship to Red Grange?

Q14   Red wasn't the only member of the Grange family signed by the Bears. Name the brother of the Ghost who came to the team from the University of Illinois.

Q15   Veteran George Trafton is recognized as the first center to originate this move in the NFL. For what is Trafton known?

CHICAGO BEARS

A1   Beattie Feathers (1,004 yards in 1934)

A2   Bill George (1952)

A3   Guard Glen Holloway (1970)

A4   Roland Harper (1975)

A5   Quarterback Paddy Driscoll

A6   Healey was the first player purchased by the Bears. (His contract was bought from the Rock Island Independents for $100, which was double the cost of a franchise at that time, 1922.)

A7   The "Wheaton Iceman" (He worked summers hauling blocks of ice in that suburb.)

A8   The Chicago Cardinals (November 26, 1925: Grange was held to 36 yards in the 0–0 game.)

A9   He received a percentage of the gate.

A10   Team: The New York Yankees
League: The American Football League (The league folded after only one season.)

A11   Bronko Nagurski

A12   Harold

A13   C. C. (Cash & Carry) Pyle was the agent who negotiated a $100,000 deal on Grange's behalf in 1924.

A14   Garland "Gardie" Grange

A15   Trafton was the first center to snap the ball with one hand.

THE UNIFORMS

Q16 Due to the number of players called into World War II, the Bears brought Bronko Nagurski back for one more season. What position did the 34-year-old play for most of the season?

Q17 What career did Bronko Nagurski pursue after he left the Bears in 1937?

Q18 Beattie Feathers was knocked out of the 1934 season with a separated shoulder. Name the Chicago Cardinal who laid the star running back out.

Q19 Chicago held the eighth overall pick in the 1939 draft, and the team knew it had no chance to select Sid Luckman. Who held the first overall pick, and what did the Bears give up to acquire it?

Q20 Who were the second- and third-string quarterbacks behind Sid Luckman in 1948?

Q21 In the 1940 season opener, this Bear fielded his first kickoff in league competition and returned it for a 93-yard TD against the Packers. Who made this auspicious debut?

Q22 Who was the only Bear to lose his life in World War II?

Q23 What Bear fullback defected to the fledgling San Francisco 49ers of the All-American Football Conference in 1946?

Q24 An end on both sides of the ball, this former Chicago Cardinal and Chicago Bear was the last man to play without a helmet. Who was he?

Q25 What AFC club attempted to lure Bobby Layne away from the Bears in 1948?

Q26 To what club did George Halas sell Bobby Layne for $50,000 and two draft choices?

Q27 Name the running back who led the 1950 Bears in rushing (571 yards).

Q28 What 1951 University of Mississippi rookie ended up as the Bears' leading rusher with 670 yards?

Q29 In order to shore up a deteriorating running game, the 1952 Bears coaxed a former Cardinal to finish his career with the North Side club. Who was he?

Q30 What Bear led the club in rushing yards for the 1952 and 1953 seasons, but did not run for more than 400 yards in either year?

CHICAGO BEARS

A16 Tackle

A17 Professional wrestling

A18 Tackle Lou Gordon

A19 The Pittsburgh Pirates received Eggs Manske in the deal.

A20 Johnny Lujack
Bobby Layne

A21 George McAfee (Later in the same game, he threw a TD pass and rushed nine yards for another score.)

A22 Young Bussey

A23 Norm Standlee

A24 Dick Plasman (1937–47)

A25 The Baltimore Colts

A26 The New York Bulldogs (1948)

A27 George Gulyanics

A28 John "Kayo" Dottley

A29 Babe Dimancheff

A30 Curley Morrison

Q31 In 1953, this Bear QB led the league in pass completions (169), set a club mark for attempts (362), and threw 24 interceptions in his only full year as Chicago's starter. Name him.

Q32 In 1954, the Bears stunned the 49ers when they scored with just a few ticks on the clock to pull out a victory, 31–27. The decisive score was a halfback option pass. What tandem connected on the play?

Q33 A trio of quarterbacks from the Bears' 1954 roster were known as the "Three B's." Who were they?

Q34 The last game of the 1956 season pitted the Bears against Detroit, and although both teams hired policemen to guard their benches, brawls occurred on the field and in the stands. What Bear knocked Detroit QB Bobby Layne out of the game with a concussion?

Q35 In 1956, the Bears spoiled Johnny Unitas's debut in the NFL when they beat the Colts, 58–27. What Chicago defensive back picked off the first pass ever thrown by the future Hall of Famer?

Q36 Unitas made his debut only because of an injury to the Colts' starting QB in the second quarter. Who opened the game for Baltimore that day?

Q37 A last-second victory over the Vikings was the highlight of the 1962 season. The Bears kicked the game-winning field goal after this player recovered a Minnesota fumble. Name the game's hero.

Q38 Who replaced the backfield combo of Rick Casares and Willie Galimore when they were both injured during the '62 season?

Q39 The 1963 season was determined by a Chicago victory over the visiting Packers, 26–7. Who laid a devastating hit on Herb Adderly on the opening kickoff to set the tone for the game?

Q40 The Bears clinched the 1963 conference title with a 24–14 win against Detroit. What Chicago cornerback intercepted a Lion pass and returned it for a 39-yard touchdown?

Q41 Name the father and son who played for the Bears in 1932 and 1964, respectively.

Q42 Name the two Bears who were killed in a July 1964 auto accident as they returned to training camp to make an 11:00 curfew.

Q43 As a free agent signee, this running back was coached by former Bear Beattie Feathers at Wake Forest, where he led the nation in rushing and scoring in his senior year (1964). Who was he?

CHICAGO BEARS

A31   George Blanda

A32   Ed Brown's 40-yard bomb went to end Harlon Hill. (Hill had four TD receptions in the game.)

A33   Zeke Bratkowski
George Blanda
Ed Brown

A34   Ed Meadows (Chicago won, 38–21.)

A35   J. C. Caroline

A36   George Shaw

A37   Ed O'Bradovich (Viking fullback Doug Mayberry fumbled on the Minnesota 20 yard line with less than 30 seconds left. Chicago won, 31–30.)

A38   Rookie Ronnie Bull
Joe Marconi (acquired from the Rams)

A39   J. C. Caroline

A40   Dave Whitsell (The Earl Morrall toss was intended for end Gail Cogdill.)

A41   Johnny Sisk (HB; 1932–36)
John Sisk (DB; 1964)

A42   Willie Galimore
Bo Farrington

A43   Brian Piccolo

Q44 Who did Dick Butkus replace as the Bears' middle linebacker when he entered the league in 1965?

Q45 In a play that became an instant part of Bear folklore, Dick Butkus chased this Detroit player out of bounds and into the stands in a 1970 game. Who was this Lion on the run?

Q46 Over his stellar 13-year career, this Hall of Famer appeared in the Pro Bowl seven consecutive times as an offensive guard. He was then switched to defensive tackle, where he played the remainder of his years. Name this two-way standout.

Q47 In the second game of his career, Gale Sayers scored the first of his 56 lifetime TDs on an 18-yard scamper. Against what team did he start the streak?

Q48 On December 12, 1965, rookie Gale Sayers equaled an NFL record by scoring six TDs in a game. Who did the Bears defeat on that day?

Q49 The last of Sayers's TDs on December 12, 1965, set a new NFL record for touchdowns in a season. What two players previously held the mark at 20 TDs?

Q50 Gale Sayers won the 1966 rushing title with 1,231 yards. Who was the last halfback to top the league in rushing?

Q51 Who replaced Gale Sayers as the Bears' kickoff return specialist in 1968?

Q52 The injury that ultimately cut short Sayers's career occurred on November 10, 1968, in a game against the 49ers. Name the defensive back who caused the knee injury.

Q53 In 1971, the Bears determined that Sayers's football future was limited, so the club drafted a back and traded for another. What pair of runners came to Chicagoland?

Q54 Who broke Gale Sayers's single-season TD record in 1975, 10 years after the Bear great set the mark?

Q55 Name the fourth-string quarterback who started five games for the Bears in 1968 and won four of them before a broken ankle knocked him out for the season.

CHICAGO BEARS

A44   Bill George

A45   Altie Taylor

A46   Stan Jones

A47   The Rams, in Los Angeles

A48   The San Francisco 49ers (61–20 at Wrigley Field)

A49   Lenny Moore (1964)
Jim Brown (1965; Brown had tied the record a week before Sayers
    broke it.)

A50   Philadelphia Eagle Steve Van Buren (1949)

A51   Cecil Turner

A52   Kermit Alexander

A53   Joe Moore (No. 1 pick, University of Missouri)
Cyril Pinder (from the Eagles)
(Neither back lasted longer than two seasons with the team.)

A54   O. J. Simpson (1975: 23 touchdowns)

A55   Virgil Carter

Q56 The Bears' top draftee in 1968 was a USC fullback who carried the ball only 12 times for 22 yards in his rookie season. After four undistinguished years, he left the club. Name him.

Q57 The Bears' victory over the Vikings in the third game of the 1968 season was a costly one, as Chicago lost two quarterbacks to injury. What three QBs played in Minnesota that day?

Q58 Identify the three quarterbacks who saw action for the Bears during the 1969 season.

Q59 Brian Piccolo died of cancer on June 16, 1970, exactly seven months after he played in his last game for the Bears. What team did he go up against on that date?

Q60 What Bear led the 1970 team in rushing with a paltry 229 yards?

Q61 Jack Concannon was tagged with a nickname, fashioned after "Broadway Joe" Namath, that was reflective of Chicago. What was it?

Q62 What player inspired the 46 defense?

Q63 What Bear was the first black football captain at Harvard (1975)?

Q64 Who was the Bears' starting signal caller for nine games during the 1975 season?

Q65 What do Dan Rives, Larry Ely, and Tom Hicks have in common?

Q66 Walter Payton was the first running back chosen in the top round of the 1975 draft and the fourth player selected overall. Name the three players who were picked ahead of Sweetness.

Q67 Walter Payton did not garner any rookie postseason honors. What two players were named all-rookie runners after the 1975 season?

Q68 What was noteworthy about Payton's selection as league MVP in 1977?

Q69 What baseball superstar did Walter Payton nose out for the 1977 UPI Athlete of the Year?

Q70 Against what club did Walter Payton establish a single-game rushing record of 275 yards?

Q71 In 1980, after only his sixth pro season, Walter Payton became the Bears' all-time leading rusher. What player did he pass in the record books?

CHICAGO BEARS

A56   Mike Hull

A57   Jack Concannon (broken collarbone—lost for seven games)
Rudy Bukich (shoulder separation—out for the season)
Larry Rakestraw

A58   Jack Concannon
Virgil Carter
Bobby Douglass

A59   The Falcons at Atlanta (November 16, 1969)

A60   Ross Montgomery

A61   "State Street" Jack

A62   Doug Plank (who wore the number)

A63   Dan Jiggets

A64   Gary Huff

A65   At various times, the trio played the middle linebacker position after Dick Butkus retired and before Mike Singletary became a fixture on the team. (Rives: 1973–75; Ely: 1975; Hicks: 1976–80)

A66   Steve Bartkowski
Randy White
Ken Huff

A67   Mike Thomas (Washington)
Don Hardeman (Houston)

A68   At 23, he was the NFL's youngest MVP.

A69   Steve Carlton

A70   The Minnesota Vikings (November 20, 1977)

A71   Gale Sayers (9,435 yards)

THE UNIFORMS

Q72   Against what team did Walter Payton break Jim Brown's NFL career rushing record of 12,312 yards in 1984?

Q73   Off what quarterback did Gary Fencik make his first pro interception?

Q74   Who replaced Rusty Lisch as the top QB on Notre Dame's 1977 national championship season?

Q75   What backfield star was voted Chicago's pro athlete of 1978?

Q76   What player was the first overall selection in the 1972 draft, was signed as a free agent six years later by the Bears, and was cut before he played in a Chicago regular-season game?

Q77   Who opened the 1979 regular season at quarterback for Chicago?

Q78   What future Hall of Famer tumbled 45 feet from a tree, broke both legs and an arm, and was confined to a wheelchair for six months when he was in fifth grade?

Q79   Brian Baschnagel hauled in his first touchdown pass against the Vikings during the 1979 season. Who threw the 54-yarder to Baschnagel?

Q80   What former Bear taught an accredited course on windsurfing at Stanford?

Q81   Who edged out Keith Van Horne for the Outland Award (for top interior lineman) in 1980?

Q82   Keith Van Horne's first game as a starter was on October 4, 1981, at Minnesota. Whom did he replace at tackle?

Q83   Mike Singletary did not start as the Bears' middle linebacker in his rookie season (1981). Who beat him out?

Q84   What two kickers filled in for the injured Bob Thomas when he was lost for the 1981 season?

Q85   With 30 seconds remaining in the game and the ball on the Green Bay one yard line, this player fumbled and cost the Bears a victory in the 1981 season opener. Who was the goat of the game?

Q86   Who did Steve McMichael replace on the Bears' defensive line when he joined the team as a free agent in 1981?

Q87   James Scott left the Bears after the 1980 season, but returned to play for Chicago in 1982. Where did he play pro ball in 1981?

CHICAGO BEARS

A72 The New Orleans Saints (October 7)

A73 Joe Namath

A74 Joe Montana

A75 Roland Harper

A76 Walt Patulski (drafted first by Buffalo)

A77 Mike Phipps

A78 Dan Hampton

A79 Walter Payton

A80 Ken Margerum

A81 Mark May

A82 Dan Jiggets

A83 Lee Kunz

A84 Hans Nielsen (He lost the job after three games.)
John Roveto

A85 Matt Suhey

A86 Brad Shearer

A87 In Montreal, with the Alouettes of the CFL

Q88 What position did Jim McMahon initially play at Brigham Young?

Q89 Whose record for career pass efficiency did Jim McMahon surpass at BYU?

Q90 Jim McMahon was the fifth overall pick in the 1982 draft and the second quarterback selected in the top five. What QB was chosen ahead of McMahon?

Q91 Identify the five quarterbacks who saw action for the Bears over the course of the 1984 season.

Q92 What type of specialist did Jim McMahon call in before the Super Bowl to treat the pain he was experiencing from his bruised buttocks?

Q93 Name the linebacker who played with the semipro Columbia Metros and the West Virginia Rockets of the American Football Association and was discovered by the Bears in one of his semipro game films.

Q94 Richard Dent, an eighth-round draft choice, made his first pro start against Philadelphia in the eighth game of the 1983 season. Who did he replace in the lineup?

Q95 Identify the Bear safety who was drafted by baseball's Toronto Blue Jays, but opted for a career in pro football instead.

Q96 Name the Bear quarterback who was offered scholarships in four different sports: golf, tennis, baseball, and football.

Q97 Name the quarterback who was a Bear for one game—the 1984 season finale—and led Chicago to a victory over the Lions in Detroit.

Q98 Who broke Neal Anderson's rushing record at the University of Florida?

Q99 What is Neal Anderson's real first name?

Q100 Who did Dave Duerson replace in the defensive backfield in 1985?

Q101 Against what team did William Perry make his rushing debut in October 1985?

Q102 Against what NFL team did the Fridge score his first rushing touchdown?

CHICAGO BEARS

A88 Punter

A89 Danny White's (McMahon: 156.9; White: 148.9)

A90 Art Schlicter (by the Baltimore Colts)

A91 Jim McMahon
Steve Fuller
Rusty Lisch
Bob Avellini
Greg Landry
(Walter Payton also played some emergency single-wing QB that
season.)

A92 An acupuncturist

A93 Dan Rains

A94 Dan Hampton (His twisted knee and subsequent surgery kept him out of
the starting lineup.)

A95 Todd Krumm

A96 Steve Fuller

A97 Greg Landry

A98 Emmitt Smith

A99 Charles

A100 Todd Bell

A101 The San Francisco 49ers

A102 The Green Bay Packers (The Bears won the Monday night game, 23–7,
on October 21, 1985.)

Q103 Tom Thayer played 46 professional football games in 1985–86—23 with the Super Bowl Bears and 23 as a member of a USFL team. With what USFL club did Thayer play?

Q104 Mark Bortz was the first Chicago guard in 36 years to play in the Pro Bowl when he was selected in 1988. Who was the last guard before Bortz to play in the annual affair?

Q105 Mike Singletary was one of two players selected unanimously to the Pro Bowl following the 1988 season. Who else was so honored?

Q106 The Bears' 1988 seventh-round draft choice was the first player selected in the World League of American Football's draft of 1991. Name the offensive lineman.

Q107 All of the members of the 1988 Michigan offensive line were drafted, including this recently retired Bear. Name him.

Q108 What Bear was named to the NFL Team of the 1980s by the Pro Football Hall of Fame Board of Selectors?

Q109 Tom Thayer did not miss a single play in the 1989 season because of injury. How many times was he flagged for holding during that time?

Q110 What Bear linebacker worked as a lumberjack for two years before entering Livingston College?

Q111 What is Trace Armstrong's given name?

Q112 Football is a family tradition for the Stonebreaker clan. Mike, who played his college ball with Notre Dame, was the Bears' ninth-round selection in the 1991 draft. For what team did Stonebreaker's father, Steve, play linebacker in the mid-sixties?

Q113 Name the two Bears who have played in three separate decades.

Q114 Name the two kickers who attended the same high school, Redan, in Stone Mountain, Georgia.

Q115 The Chicago 6 rock band is made up of four present and past Bears as well as two former Blackhawks. Name the group members.

Q116 What Bear went to the same high school as Richard Nixon?

CHICAGO BEARS

A103 The Chicago Blitz

A104 Stan Jones (1952)

A105 Reggie White

A106 Caesar Rentie (Rentie was with the Bears for only one season. He was chosen by the WLAF's New York—New Jersey Knights.)

A107 Kurt Becker

A108 Mike Singletary

A109 He was never penalized for that infraction.

A110 Steve Hyche

A111 Raymond

A112 The Baltimore Colts (1964–66)

A113 Sid Luckman (1939–51)
Dan Hampton (1979–90)

A114 Kevin Butler
Chris Gardocki

A115 Bears: Shaun Gayle, Dave Duerson, Otis Wilson, and Dan Hampton
Blackhawks: Curt Fraser and Gary Nyland

A116 Keith Van Horne (Fullerton High in California)

THE UNIFORMS

Q117 What Bear great attended Chicago Vocational High, the same school from which Chris Zorich graduated?

Q118 Name the Bear whose aunt is Academy Award winner Olympia Dukakis.

Q119 Who is the only player in NFL history to be selected three times to both the offensive and defensive All-Pro teams in the same year?

Q120 Who is the only NFLer besides the Chicago player cited above to be selected to both the offensive and defensive All-Pro teams in the same year?

Q121 Name the six Bears who were named to the 1963 All-Pro team.

Q122 What three Bears were enshrined in the Pro Football Hall of Fame as charter members when the facility officially opened in 1963?

Q123 In 1991, for the first time in a decade, the Bears had a quarterback—Jim Harbaugh—start all 16 games in a season. Who was the last QB prior to Harbaugh to do this?

Q124 Identify the Bear who is the son-in-law of Hall of Famer Gino Cappelletti, the former AFLer who played 11 seasons for the Boston Patriots.

Q125 Match the player with his retired uniform number.
(A) George Halas   3
(B) Red Grange   5
(C) Bronko Nagurski   7
(D) Willie Galimore   28
(E) Bill George   34
(F) Bill Hewitt   41
(G) Sid Luckman   42
(H) George McAfee   56
(I) Walter Payton   61
(J) Brian Piccolo   77

Q126 The previous question lists 10 of the 11 Bears whose numbers have been retired by the club. What player is missing?

CHICAGO BEARS

A117   Dick Butkus (Keena Turner also attended the school.)

A118   Chris Zorich

A119   George O'Connor of the Bears (1951–53: offensive tackle and linebacker)

A120   Detroit's Leon Hart (1951)

A121   Mike Ditka
Richie Petitbon
Joe Fortunato
Bill George
Doug Atkins
Rosey Taylor

A122   George Halas
Red Grange
Bronko Nagurski

A123   Vince Evans

A124   Tom Waddle

A125

A – 7	F – 56
B – 77	G – 42
C – 3	H – 5
D – 28	I – 34
E – 61	J – 41

A126   No. 66—Bulldog Turner

SETTING THE STANDARD

Q1 What is the longest consecutive losing streak sustained by the Bears?

Q2 The shortest overtime game in league history took place on Thanksgiving Day, 1980, when the Bears mashed the Lions, 23–17, with only 21 seconds gone in the extra period. Who returned the kickoff 95 yards to end the game?

Q3 The 1933–34 Bears and the 1941–42 Bears put together win streaks of 18 consecutive games. Name the two other clubs that have reached the same plateau.

Q4 What team demolished the Bears by a 52–0 score, Chicago's biggest margin of defeat?

Q5 The Bears' largest margin of victory occurred on December 8, 1940. Who did they annihilate by a 73–0 score?

Q6 Name the Bear who became the first pro to throw for more than 400 yards in a game.

Q7 Who is the only Chicago quarterback to pass for more than 2,000 yards in a season three times?

Q8 What tandem hooked up on an 89-yard bomb on September 21, 1980, for the longest Bear TD pass in Soldier Field history?

Q9 What Chicago quarterback posted the best passing rating (80.1) by a rookie?

Q10 Name the Bear who set an NFL record for most yards rushing by a quarterback in one season, with 968 yards in 1972.

Q11 Name the Bear QB who led the NFL in 1980 with eight rushing touchdowns.

Q12 What Bear tied an NFL record with 14 receptions in a game during the 1949 season?

Q13 Name the Chicago end who tied an all-time Bear record in 1961 when he took a pass 98 yards for a touchdown.

Q14 Though the team suffered through a dismal season in 1964, this Bear receiver set club records for receptions (93) and receiving yardage (1,200). Who was this pacesetter?

CHICAGO BEARS

A1   Eight games (twice: December 15, 1968—November 2, 1969; September 25, 1978—November 12, 1978)

A2   Dave Williams

A3   Miami Dolphins (1972–73)
San Franscisco 49ers (1989–90)

A4   The Baltimore Colts (9/27/64)

A5   The Washington Redskins

A6   Sid Luckman (11/14/43: vs. Giants; 433 yards)

A7   Bill Wade

A8   Vince Evans to Rickey Watts (against Minnesota, which won, 34–14)

A9   Jim McMahon (His rating was the best in league history.)

A10   Bobby Douglass

A11   Vince Evans

A12   End Jim Keane (in a game won by the Giants, 35–28)

A13   John "Bo" Farrington (vs. Detroit)

A14   Johnny Morris

*** BEAR FAST FACTS ***

Walter Payton is the NFL's all-time receiver among running backs, with 492 receptions.

SETTING THE STANDARD

Q15   Richard Dent is the Bears' leader of the sack. He set the club's season mark with 17.5 takedowns in 1985 and four years later became Chicago's all-time leader. Whose record did he smash?

Q16   Whose team record did Mark Carrier eclipse when he intercepted 10 passes during the 1990 season?

Q17   Identify the Bear who set a single season rushing record for average yards (9.94; 1,004 yards).

Q18   Who holds the club record for the longest punt return?

Q19   What Bear holds the team record for the longest kickoff return?

Q20   What Bear equaled an NFL record in 1971 with four kickoff returns that resulted in TDs?

Q21   Name the two Bears who have led the NFL in kickoff returns.

Q22   Name the Bear kicker who set a club standard in 1961 when he nailed five field goals in a game against Detroit.

Q23   What Minnesota kicker hit five field goals in a game against the Bears in 1973?

Q24   What rookie put his name in the record books for the longest punt return in franchise history when he scampered 95 yards for a TD in the 1990 season finale against Kansas City?

Q25   What Bear free agent set a team record for most career safeties, with three?

Q26   The Bears have the unfortunate distinction of being on the wrong end of record-setting scores twice, as the Chicagoans gave up 52 points on two separate occasions. What team lists the Bears in its club record book as the opponent that gave up the most points in a game?

CHICAGO BEARS

A15   Jim Osborne's

A16   Roosevelt Taylor's (nine in 1963)

A17   Beattie Feathers (1934)

A18   Scooter McLean (1942: 89 yards)

A19   Gale Sayers (1967: 103 years)

A20   Cecil Turner (He tied Packer Travis Williams's 1967 mark.)

A21   Walter Payton (1975)
          Dennis Gentry (1986)

A22   Roger Leclerc (The Lions eked out a win, 16–15.)

A23   Fred Cox (9/23/73)

A24   Johnny Bailey (K.C. beat the Bears, 21–10, dealing Chicago its only
          home defeat of the season.)

A25   Steve McMichael

A26   The San Francisco 49ers (1965 and 1992)

*** BEAR FAST FACTS ***

Jim Harbaugh established a team record when he threw 173
consecutive passes without an interception during the 1990 season.
He eclipsed Jim McMahon's mark of 134 straight tosses without a
theft (1984).

Q1 The Bears played in the top-rated "Monday Night Football" game of all time (a 29.6 rating on December 2, 1985). Who did Chicago share the national spotlight with that night?

Q2 By what names was the franchise known before the team was christened the "Bears"?

Q3 The forerunner of the NFL, the American Professional Football Association, was formed in 1920. What were the names of Chicago's two franchises?

Q4 The Bears are one of only two original franchises still in existence. What is the other?

Q5 The first indoor game at Chicago Stadium was an exhibition that pitted the Bears against the Cardinals. For what cause was the 1930 game staged?

Q6 The longest TD play at Soldier Field occurred during a 1985 Bear-Patriot matchup. What two players hooked up on the play?

Q7 What was Soldier Field known as when the 45,000-seat stadium opened in 1924?

Q8 When did the Bears change their address to Soldier Field?

Q9 Why did NFL commissioner Joe Carr fine the Bears, Packers, and Portsmouth Spartans in 1931?

Q10 What *Chicago Tribune* sports editor conceived of the idea in 1934 of the College All-Star Game?

Q11 The College All-Star Game, which ran from 1934 through 1976, matched the best college players against an NFL team. Name the only pro club to appear in the annual game more times than Chicago.

Q12 The concept of the College All-Star Game was designed to lend credence and prestige to pro football. What was unique about the first preseason classic involving the Bears?

Q13 The Bears played the College All-Stars in 1935 at Soldier Field. Two of the collegians would attain fame, one in politics and the other in show business. Who are they?

Q14 When did the Bears play their first Thanksgiving Day game?

CHICAGO BEARS

A1 The Miami Dolphins (Miami topped the Bears, 38–24.)

A2 The Decatur Staleys
The Chicago Staleys

A3 The Chicago Cardinals (or as they were known locally, the Racine Cardinals) and the Chicago Tigers (which disbanded after the 1920 season)

A4 The Phoenix Cardinals (formerly the Racine Cardinals, Chicago Cardinals, and St. Louis Cardinals)

A5 It was an exhibition for unemployment relief.

A6 New England's Tony Eason to Craig James (90 yards)

A7 Municipal Grant Park Stadium

A8 1971

A9 The teams were using players whose college classes had not graduated.

A10 Arch Ward

A11 The Green Bay Packers (They appeared in eight games to Chicago's seven.)

A12 It was the only game to result in a scoreless tie.

A13 Politics: Gerald Ford (Michigan center)
Show biz: Irv Kupcinet (North Dakota QB)

A14 1934 (The Bears prevailed over the Lions, 19–16.)

Q15 In 1946, the financial security of the Bears was severely threatened by the introduction of another Chicago football team. What was the name of the All-American Football Conference entry?

Q16 The Bears' 5–7 mark in 1952 was the second-worst record in the NFL. The only team with a more dismal record was an expansion franchise that lasted for only a single season. What was the name of the now defunct club?

Q17 In what year did the Bears' crosstown rivals, the Cardinals, relocate to St. Louis?

Q18 What expansion team defeated the Bears in the 1961 season opener?

Q19 Who did the Bears play on November 24, 1963, the weekend of President Kennedy's assassination?

Q20 Why did NFL commissioner Pete Rozelle suspend the six officials who called a 1968 game between the Bears and Rams?

Q21 Identify the only team that Chicago defeated in its 1969 1–13 season.

Q22 Who did the Bears meet in their last game played at Wrigley Field, on December 13, 1970?

Q23 Name the Detroit Lion wide receiver who collapsed during a 1970 game against the Bears and died shortly afterward.

Q24 The Bears got off on the right cleat when they won the first game they ever played at Soldier Field. Who did they defeat on September 19, 1971?

Q25 In what year did the Bears last post a losing record at home?

Q26 In order to enter the playoffs for the first time in 14 years, the Bears needed a victory in the last game of the 1977 season. What team did they edge in overtime, 12–9, to earn the berth?

Q27 Who was the only Bear to cross the goal line in that 1977 season-finale victory?

Q28 In the game cited above, a Chicago kicker launched the winning field goal with less than 12 seconds left in the extra period. Who nailed the 27-yarder?

CHICAGO BEARS

A15 The Chicago Rockets

A16 The Dallas Texans (They were the last team to drop out of the NFL.)

A17 1960

A18 The Minnesota Vikings (behind rookie QB Fran Tarkenton)

A19 The Pittsburgh Steelers (The game ended in a 17–17 tie.)

A20 With the Bears leading 17–16, the officials turned the ball over to Chicago in the waning moments of the fourth quarter, but the Rams had had only three official downs. (The error and loss cost L.A. its chance at the Coastal Division crown.)

A21 The Pittsburgh Steelers (That win cost Chicago the first overall pick in the 1970 draft.)

A22 The Green Bay Packers (Chicago won, 35–17.)

A23 Chuck Hughes

A24 The Pittsburgh Steelers (17–15)

A25 1975 (3–4)

A26 The Giants

A27 Robin Earl

A28 Bob Thomas (The victory was the first OT win in Chicago history.)

*** BEAR FAST FACTS ***

The Bears and the Phoenix Cardinals were the only two NFL teams that did not invest in the WLAF's inaugural season.

Q29 The final game of the 1979 season was marred by the death of a team executive. Who passed away prior to the Bears game with the Cardinals?

Q30 What team's loss on the final day of the 1979 regular season allowed the Bears to back into the playoffs?

Q31 What club did Chicago pummel 44–0 in 1985, ending that franchise's record of 218 straight games without a shutout?

Q32 What is the "Mark Carrier Rule"?

Q33 On November 25, 1990, the Bears were one of six NFL divisional leaders that lost. Name the other five clubs that went down to defeat that weekend.

Q34 The Bears defeated only one team with a winning record during the 1990 season. Who did they edge, 9–7, in the season opener?

Q35 Name the three foreign sites in which the Bears have played exhibition games.

Q36 What team has never defeated the Bears in 10 preseason encounters?

Q37 Only two teams have posted longer consecutive home winning records than the Bears. Who are they?

Q38 In what year was the song "Bear Down, Chicago Bears" introduced?

Q39 For a fee of $100 each. George Halas and 123 other team representatives formed a league that was the precursor to the NFL. What was the name of the league?

GLORY DAYS

Q1 Due to a first-place tie, the league arranged for the first playoff game in NFL history. Who did the Bears play for the crown?

Q2 What was unique about the championship-game matchup of 1933?

Q3 In the Chicag—New York 1933 title game, the Bears were trailing the Giants by five points in the fourth quarter when Bronko Nagurski threw a pass to Bill Hewitt. Hewitt lateraled the ball to a teammate, who ran 19 yards to pay dirt. Who scored the winning TD?

CHICAGO BEARS

A29   Bear president Mugs Halas

A30   The Washington Redskins (35–34 to Dallas)

A31   The Dallas Cowboys (November 17)

A32   The "rule" refers to Commissioner Paul Tagliabue's approval of the Bears' signing of Carrier on draft day 1990, after the team had negotiated with three players and chose one they knew would be in training camp on time.

A33   NFC—East: Giants (31–13 loss to the Eagles)
         West: 49ers (lost 28–17 to the Rams)
AFC—East: Bills (27–24 loss to Houston)
         Central: Bengals (34–20 losers to the Colts)
         West: Raiders (27–24 losers to the Chiefs)
(The Bears lost to the Vikings 41–13.)

A34   The Seattle Seahawks

A35   Berlin (vs. the 49ers; 1991)
Gothenburg, Sweden (vs. the Vikings; 1988)
London (vs. the Cowboys; 1986)

A36   The Buffalo Bills (0–9–1)

A37   Washington Redskins
Pittsburgh Steelers

A38   1941 (at the championship game)

A39   The American Professional Football Association

A1   The Portsmouth Spartans (Chicago won, 9–0, on a two-yard pass from Nagurski to Grange.)

A2   The game was unique for two reasons: It marked the first NFL championship game scheduled before the season, and it was the first championship game that matched division winners, Chicago from the Western Division and the Giants of the Eastern Division.

A3   Bill Karr (The Bears won, 23–21.)

Q4 Undefeated in 13 regular-season games, the Bears met the Giants for the 1934 championship at New York's Polo Grounds. Who scored Chicago's only touchdown of the game?

Q5 Despite being beaten twice by the Bears in the regular season and trailing 13–3 in the third quarter, the Giants went on to win the '34 championship game, 30–13. What turned the title match around?

Q6 Who kicked two field goals and an extra point for the Bears in the 1934 championship contest?

Q7 What two Hall of Famers played their last game for Chicago in the 1934 championship?

Q8 After the 1934 championship game, the Bears and Giants played an exhibition game in Los Angeles. Who won the contest?

Q9 The 1937 NFL championship was played between Chicago and Washington at Wrigley Field. What unusual apparel were both teams wearing?

Q10 Who scored two touchdowns for Chicago in its 28–21 loss to the Redskins in the 1937 championships?

Q11 The 1940 Bears hold the NFL record for the most interceptions in a single game in postseason play. How many thefts did the Bears commit?

Q12 How many Bears scored touchdowns during Chicago's 73–0 rout of the Redskins in the 1940 championship game?

Q13 The 1940 championship game was the first contest to be carried on network radio (Mutual Broadcasting System). Who was behind the microphone for the historic broadcast?

Q14 The first divisional playoff game took place in 1941, when the Bears were tied for the Western Conference title. Who did Chicago meet?

Q15 In the Bears' 37–9 victory over the Giants in the 1941 championship game, one Chicago player accounted for two TDs and rushed for more yardage (89 yards) than the entire New York team. Who was he?

Q16 Despite averaging 34 points per game during the regular season, Chicago could manage only one TD in its 1942 championship-game loss to Washington (14–6). Who returned a Redskin fumble 50 yards for the Bears' only score?

CHICAGO BEARS

A4   Bronko Nagurski

A5   The New York players donned sneakers for the second half, while the Bears "skated" on the icy field with their football cleats.

A6   Jack Manders

A7   Red Grange
Roy "Link" Lyman

A8   Chicago (21–0)

A9   Sneakers (The frozen field and the 1934 Bears–Giant game had taught teams a lesson.)

A10   Jack Manders

A11   Eight (vs. Washington, 1940: 73–0)

A12   10 (11 TDs were recorded.)

A13   Red Barber

A14   The Green Bay Packers (Chicago came out on top, 33–14.)

A15   Norm Standlee

A16   Lee Artoe

Q17 During the 1943 championship game against Washington, a Bear official ejected an unwelcome visitor from the Chicago bench. Who was on the Bears' sideline?

Q18 Prior to the 1946 championship game, two Giants were accused of taking money from gamblers for the purpose of throwing the game. Who were the players on the take?

Q19 Chicago's 24–14 win over New York in the 1946 championship game was highlighted by a 39-yard interception return for a TD. Name the Bear who corralled the errant pass.

Q20 The Bears were tied by the Rams for the 1950 conference championship, and the two clubs met in a playoff game at the Coliseum. Who scored three times to lead L.A. to a 24–14 win?

Q21 The Giants humbled Chicago, 47–7, in the 1956 NFL championship game. Who was the only Bear to cross the goal line that day?

Q22 Quarterback Bill Wade led the Bears to the 1963 NFL title at Wrigley Field. What team did the Bears thump, 14–10, and what QB did the champs intercept five times?

Q23 In the just cited playoff encounter with the Giants, this Chicago linebacker put a lick on Y. A. Tittle that temporarily knocked him out of the game. It was after the quarterback returned that he threw those five interceptions. Who laid the vicious hit on the "Bald Eagle"?

Q24 Whose interception with 10 seconds remaining in the 1963 championship game secured the Bears' victory?

Q25 Who walked away with the team's game ball after the 1963 championship game?

Q26 The Bears secured their first playoff appearance in 14 years when this kicker nailed a 28-yard field goal with nine seconds remaining in a 1977 OT game with the Giants. Who booted the three-pointer?

Q27 What team, bound for the Super Bowl, ruined the Bears' postseason with a 37–7 thrashing in the 1977 divisional playoff?

Q28 This signal caller threw a TD pass to Steve Schubert against Dallas in 1977. It marked the first Bear playoff touchdown in 31 years. What Chicago QB completed the play?

Q29 Who was the only Bear to score a touchdown in the 1977 divisional playoff?

CHICAGO BEARS

A17 George Preston Marshall (owner of the Redskins)

A18 Fullback Merle Hapes
Quarterback Frank Filchock
(Hapes and Filchock were suspended for an indefinite period after the game.)

A19 Dante Magnini

A20 Tom Fears (on receptions of 43, 68, and 27 yards, each on a pass from Bob Waterfield)

A21 Rick Casares

A22 The Bears intercepted five Y. A. Tittle passes en route to their victory over the Giants.

A23 Larry Morris

A24 Richie Petitbon

A25 Defensive coach George Allen

A26 Bob Thomas (The Bears won, 12–9.)

A27 The Dallas Cowboys (who won the Super Bowl that year)

A28 Bob Avellini

A29 Steve Schubert (on a 34-yard pass from Bob Avellini)

Q30   Who had three interceptions in the 1977 postseason contest?

Q31   In the third quarter of the 1979 divisional playoffs, Chicago marched to the Eagles' nine yard line. Who thwarted the drive with an interception in the end zone?

Q32   A penalty in the third quarter wiped out an 84-yard Walter Payton run that could have won the 1979 playoff game for Chicago. What were the Bears flagged for?

Q33   After beating Washington 23–19 in the 1984 divisional playoffs, the Bears lost to the 49ers in the NFC title game, 23–0. Name the last team shut out in the NFC championship game prior to the Bears.

Q34   In the second quarter of the 1984 divisional playoffs, Walter Payton put the Bears ahead when he tossed a 19-yard TD pass. Who was on the receiving end?

Q35   The first Chicago points of the 1985 divisional game were scored when the Giants' punter missed the ball and a Bear grabbed it and ran it in for a five-yard TD. Who gave Chicago the lead?

Q36   What Bear scooped up a Ram fumble and lumbered 52 yards for a TD in the 1985 NFC title game?

Q37   It was a sign of things to come when the Bears registered two straight shutouts in the 1985 NFC playoffs. What two teams did Chicago whitewash before it demolished New England in the Super Bowl, 46–10?

Q38   As he watched the Bears annihilate the Pats in Super Bowl XX, this network announcer commented, "If it were a fight, they'd have to stop it." Who said it?

Q39   The final points of the 1985 season came on a safety against the Pats in Super Bowl XX. Who sacked Steve Grogan for the deuce?

Q40   Who scored the only touchdown against the Bears in the entire 1985 playoffs?

Q41   The Bears lost the 1986 NFC divisional playoff to the Redskins, 27–13. Who was the only Chicago player to make it into the Washington end zone?

Q42   The 1987 divisional playoff was a repeat of the previous year's loss to the Redskins. Who scored the deciding points for Washington with a 52-yard interception return for a TD?

CHICAGO BEARS

A30 Charlie Waters of Dallas

A31 Bobby Howard

A32 Illegal motion (The run would have put the ball at the Eagle one yard line with Chicago ahead, 17–10. The Bears lost, 27–17.)

A33 Tampa Bay (1979: 9–0 vs. L.A. Rams)

A34 Pat Dunsmore

A35 Shaun Gayle (who recovered Sean Landeta's fumble)

A36 Wilber Marshall

A37 New York Giants (21–0)
Los Angeles Rams (24–0)

A38 Dick Enberg

A39 Henry Waechter

A40 Irving Fryar of the Patriots (Super Bowl XX; eight-yard pass from Steve Grogan in the fourth quarter)

A41 Willie Gault (on a 50-yard pass from McMahon)

A42 Darrell Green (Chicago fell, 21–17.)

Q43 Name the Bear signal caller who led the team to victory over the Eagles in the 1988 Fog Bowl playoff to become the only Chicago quarterback to win a postseason game since the 1985 Super Bowl year.

Q44 The 49ers captured the 1988 NFC championship with a 28–3 mauling of the Bears at Soldier Field. How many times did Chicago cross the Niners' 40 yard line?

Q45 Chicago prevailed over New Orleans, 16–6, in the 1990 NFC wild-card game. Who was responsible for the game's only touchdown?

TRADES, WAIVES, AND ACQUISITIONS

Q1 Who was the Bears' first No. 1 draft choice?

Q2 What future Hall of Fame tackle was acquired by the Bears during the 1922 season from the Rock Island Independents?

Q3 Who was the last player selected by the Bears in the NFL's first-ever draft in 1936?

Q4 The first player ever selected in the NFL draft was chosen by Philadelphia on February 8, 1936. The Eagles traded the halfback's rights to Chicago, but the Bears never signed him. Who was this Heisman Trophy winner?

Q5 Name the Bears' No. 1 choice in the 1941 draft who turned his back on Chicago and played for the AFL's New York Americans instead.

Q6 The NFL introduced a bonus choice in 1947 that allowed one team to select a collegian before the first round of the draft. Through a lottery, the Bears won the first bonus. Who was their choice?

Q7 Chicago used Pittsburgh's seventh overall pick of the 1948 draft to select Texas QB Bobby Layne. Who did the Bears give to the Steelers for the pick?

Q8 Who did the Bears choose with their own pick (13th overall) of the 1948 draft?

Q9 After trading Bobby Layne in 1948, George Halas decided he needed another third-string QB, so he selected a 21-year-old quarterback from the University of Kentucky in the 1949 draft. Name the player.

CHICAGO BEARS

A43   Mike Tomczak

A44   Twice (resulting in three points, a 25-yard field goal)

A45   James Thornton (on an 18-yard pass from Mike Tomczak in the second quarter)

A1   Joe Stydahar (tackle from West Virginia; 1936)

A2   Ed Healey

A3   Dan Fortmann of Colgate (He played with the Bears for eight seasons.)

A4   Jay Berwanger (Berwanger, from the University of Chicago, never played pro ball.)

A5   Tommy Harmon of Michigan

A6   Oklahoma A & M back Bob Fenimore

A7   Ray Evans

A8   Texas end Max Baumgardner

A9   George Blanda

TRADES, WAIVES, AND ACQUISITIONS

Q10   The Bears drafted the 1952 Heisman Trophy winner, but the back chose not to play pro ball. Who was this Princeton grad?

Q11   In 1952, the Bears drafted the first black to play for the club. Who was he?

Q12   What Hall of Famer was drafted by Cleveland in 1952 and traded to Chicago three years later for a pair of draft choices?

Q13   In 1956, the Bears drafted an Illinois running back who had broken several of Red Grange's school records. He was converted to a defensive back, where he was recognized as one of the best. Who was this two-way standout?

Q14   What Florida A & M running back was drafted by the Bears on the advice of a jockey at Miami's Hialeah racetrack?

Q15   What onetime Ram quarterback did the Bears acquire in 1961 to shore up their weak offense?

Q16   Name the punter who was acquired from Pittsburgh in 1962 and held that roster spot for 12 seasons.

Q17   What 1965 first-round draft choice was lost by the Bears to the AFL San Diego Chargers?

Q18   What fourth-round draft pick, plucked by the Bears in the 1965 draft, was lost to the Boston Patriots?

Q19   Hall of Famer Doug Atkins was traded along with offensive tackle Herman Lee to New Orleans in 1967. What Saint came to the Bears in the transaction?

Q20   What offensive lineman came to the Second City after the Bears traded Roosevelt Taylor to the 49ers in 1969?

Q21   The Bears sent their 1970 top draft pick (second overall) to the Packers. What trio of Green Bay Packers came to Chicagoland in return?

Q22   The Bears justified the 1970 trade involving their No. 1 pick because the player they coveted would almost undoubtedly be unavailable when their turn came up. What future Hall of Famer did the Bears have their eye on?

Q23   The second of the Bears' controversial 1970 trades sent Rufus Mayes to Cincinnati. What pair of defensive linemen were acquired in the deal?

CHICAGO BEARS

A10   Dick Kazmaier

A11   Eddie Macon

A12   Doug Atkins (along with Ken Gorgal)

A13   J. C. Caroline

A14   Willie Galimore (He played seven seasons with the Bears.)

A15   Bill Wade

A16   Bobby Joe Green

A17   Tennessee lineman Steve DeLong

A18   Jim Nance

A19   Don Coftcheck

A20   Howard Mudd

A21   Bob Hyland
Lee Roy Caffey
Elijah Pitts

A22   Terry Bradshaw (who was Pittsburgh's top pick)

A23   Bill Staley
Harry Gunner

TRADES, WAIVES, AND ACQUISITIONS

Q24   Who did Chicago obtain from the Pittsburgh Steelers in 1970 to fill the void left by departed third-string QB Virgil Carter?

Q25   On January 30, 1973, the Bears gave up a pair of 1973 first-round picks in two separate trades so they could acquire an experienced tight end and running back. Who came to Chicago in the deal?

Q26   Cecil Turner was sent to the 49ers in 1974 in exchange for a tight end and wide receiver. Name the twosome.

Q27   What team drafted Gary Fencik in the 10th round of the 1976 draft?

Q28   What colorful wide receiver did the Bears pick up from Dallas for a pair of draft choices in a 1978 deal with the Cowboys?

Q29   In order to draft Dan Hampton in the 1979 draft, the Bears gave up a player to obtain the fourth overall pick from Tampa Bay. Who became a Buccaneer in the transaction?

Q30   How did the Bears acquire Hall of Famer Alan Page from the Vikings early in the 1979 season?

Q31   What three players were drafted ahead of Dan Hampton in the first round of the 1979 draft?

Q32   The Bears' first- and second-round picks in the 1981 draft became fixtures on offense and defense, respectively. Who are they?

Q33   What 1982 second-round draft choice turned his back on the Bears and opted to play with the Chicago Blitz of the USFL?

Q34   Name the Bear twosome who were both chosen in the first round of the 1983 draft.

Q35   What two linebackers were chosen ahead of All-American Wilber Marshall in the 1984 draft?

Q36   What team originally drafted Mike Tomczak?

Q37   David Tate was an eighth-round 1988 draft pick out of Colorado. Whom did the Bears ship to New England for the choice?

Q38   Trace Armstrong was taken by the Bears in the first round of the 1989 draft with a pick obtained in a trade with the Redskins. What player was dispatched to Washington for the draft choice?

Q39   Who is the only cornerback ever selected by the Bears with a first-round draft choice?

CHICAGO BEARS

A24 Kent Nix

A25 Tight end Craig Cotton (from Detroit)
Back Carl Garrett (from New England)

A26 Tight end Dick Witcher
Receiver John Isenbarger

A27 The Miami Dolphins (He was cut because of injuries and illness.)

A28 Golden Richards

A29 Wally Chambers

A30 The team picked him off the waiver list.

A31 Tom Cousineau
Mike Bell
Jack Thompson

A32 Keith Van Horne (USC)
Mike Singletary (Baylor)

A33 Tim Wrightman (tight end from UCLA)

A34 Jimbo Covert (PIttsburgh; sixth overall pick)
Willie Gault (Tennessee; 18th overall selection)

A35 Carl Banks (Giants; third overall)
Rick Hunley (Bengals; seventh overall)
(Marshall was the 11th overall pick.)

A36 He was never drafted. Tomczak signed with the Bears in 1985 as an
undrafted free agent.

A37 Doug Flutie

A38 Wilber Marshall

A39 Donnell Woolford (Clemson; 1989)

TRADES, WAIVES, AND ACQUISITIONS

Q40   In what two categories did Chris Gardocki rank among the national collegiate leaders?

Q41   Name the Plan B wide receiver who almost signed with the Bears in 1991, but opted to return to the Raiders.

Q42   In a swap of defensive players, the Bears traded corner Vestee Jackson for this Miami Dolphin in the spring of 1991. Who came to Chicago in the exchange?

Q43   Who is the only Plan B free agent ever signed by the Bears?

Q44   From what school have the Bears drafted the most players?

Q45   For what position have the Bears used their No. 1 draft pick most often?

Q46   Name the seven quarterbacks selected by the Bears in the first round since the NFL draft was instituted in 1936.

CHICAGO BEARS

A40 Placekicking and punting

A41 Jamie Holland

A42 Eric Kumerow

A43 Kurt Becker (After being cut by the Bears in 1989, Becker played a season with the Rams. The Bears reacquired him prior to the 1990 campaign.)

A44 Notre Dame (34 as of 1991)

A45 Running back (23 top choices)

A46 Sid Luckman (Columbia; 1939)
Bob Williams (Notre Dame; 1951)
Frankie Albert (Stanford; 1942)
Jim McMahon (Brigham Young; 1982)
Johnny Lujack (North Dakota; 1946)
Bobby Layne (Texas; 1948)
Jim Harbaugh (Michigan; 1987)

*** BEAR FAST FACTS ***

Though the "Rozelle Rule" was implemented in 1978, Wilber Marshall was only the second player in the league to take advantage of limited free agency. (He jumped from Chicago to Washington in 1988.) The first was cornerback Norm Thompson, who moved from the Cardinals to the Colts in 1978.

Chicago Cubs

CHICAGO CUBS

CHICAGO CUBS—1945

FRONT ROW—left to right: Paul Derringer, Mickey Livingston, Stanley Hack, Roy Johnson, Milt Stock, Charlie Grimm, Jimmie Chalikis, Bat Boy—seated on ground, Len Rice, Lennie Merullo, Phil Cavarretta, Claude Passeau.

SECOND ROW—left to right: Loyd Christopher, Paul Gillespie, Don Johnson, Andy Pafko, Harry "P-Nuts" Lowrey, Bill Schuster, Eddie Sauer, Dewey Williams, Ray Prim, Harold H. Vandenberg.

BACK ROW—left to right: Paul Erickson, Frank Secory, Eddie Hanyzewski, Bill Nicholson, Hank Wyse, Andy Lotshaw, Heinz Becker, George Hennessey, Red Smith, Bob Chipman, Mack Stewart.

THE SUITS

Q1 Which Cub manager has the best won-lost record?

Q2 Of Cub managers who have led the club for a minimum of 100 games, who has the worst record?

Q3 Who is the only Chicago native to manage the Cubs?

Q4 Who was the Cubs' first general manager?

Q5 Who has had the longest tenure as the team's general manager?

Q6 What Chicago skipper once threw team owner A. G. Spalding off the field for challenging one of his decisions?

Q7 What Chicago pilot pioneered the use of platoons, signals, spring training, the hit-and-run, and a pitching rotation?

Q8 When this manager was finally let go, his fans raised $50,000 for him, but he turned the money down. Who was this beloved skipper?

Q9 The Cub franchise and the National League were established by the same man. Who was he?

Q10 The Cubs' first manager, this man won 46 games in 1876, opened a sporting goods company, and became the second owner of the Chicago franchise. Name this enterprising Hall of Famer.

Q11 On April 28, 1906, a once-in-a-lifetime occurrence took place—two major league player-managers stole home plate on the same day. Name the Cub pilot who made the move.

Q12 What Cub player-manager had the dubious distinction of being the first man to be ejected from a World Series game?

CHICAGO CUBS

A1 Frank Chance (1905–12: 778–396; .663)

A2 Joe Amalfitano (1979, 1980–81: 66–116; .363)

A3 Phil Cavarretta

A4 Charles Weeghman (1916–18)

A5 John Holland (1957–75)

A6 Cap Anson

A7 Cap Anson

A8 Cap Anson

A9 William A. Hulbert (He held the dual roles of league president and club president from 1876 until his death in 1882.)

A10 Albert G. Spalding

A11 Frank Chance (The steal propelled Chicago to a 1–0 victory over Cincinnati; Chance's counterpart that day was Pittsburgh's Fred Clarke, whose team won, 10–1.)

A12 Frank Chance (1910)

*** CUB FAST FACTS ***

THE FRIENDLY CONFINES OF WRIGLEY FIELD
Ernie Bank's Career Homers
Home—290   Away—222

*** CUB FAST FACTS ***

Chicago is the only city in America with five major league teams playing within the city limits.

Q13 Sandwiched between the managerial careers of Tinker and Evers, this player led the Cubs to a pennant during his four-year career (1917–20). Name the man who had an otherwise undistinguished career.

Q14 Name the three men who managed the Cubs during the 1925 season.

Q15 How many games were left in the 1930 season when Joe McCarthy called it quits as the Cubs' manager?

Q16 How many tenures did Charlie Grimm have as Cubs manager?

Q17 Gabby Hartnett replaced Charlie Grimm as Cub manager on July 20, 1938, after owner Philip Wrigley offered the job to (and was turned down by) one of his players. Who refused Wrigley's offer?

Q18 Jimmy Johnson was fired as Cub manager during the 1944 season, but Charlie Grimm, who was hired to succeed him, missed one game while in transit. Who was at the helm for the one contest, the shortest tenure of any Cub skipper?

Q19 This onetime Cub manager presented his wife with a wedding diamond on the diamond when he married her at a ballpark in Elmira, New York, in 1951. Who was this romantic?

Q20 How long did the "College of Coaches" manage the Cubs before the idea was dismissed?

Q21 Name the quintet who made up the College of Coaches in 1961 and 1962.

Q22 In 1963, an athletic director was hired to oversee the burgeoning College of Coaches. What was his name?

Q23 In 1963, the rotation process of the College ended, and one man assumed the head role for the next two and a half seasons. Name him.

Q24 Leo Durocher was married three times. One of his wives was a well-known actress. Name her.

Q25 Name the four teams for whom Leo "the Lip" played in his 17-year big league career.

Q26 Identify the baseball commissioner who suspended Leo Durocher from baseball in 1947.

Q27 Camp Ojibwa did little to solidify Leo Durocher's position with the Cubs in 1969. What does the Wisconsin boys camp have to do with the Chicago manager?

CHICAGO CUBS

A13   Fred Mitchell

A14   Bill Killifer
Rabbit Maranville
George Gibson

A15   Four

A16   Three (1932–38; 1944–49; 1960)

A17   William Jurges

A18   Roy "Hardrock" Johnson (He lost the game.)

A19   Don Zimmer

A20   Five Years (1961–65)

A21   1961:   Vedie Himsl (10–21)   1962:   Tappe (4–16)
Harry Craft (7–9)   Charlie Metro (43–69)
Lou Klein (5–7)   Klein (12–18)
Elvin Tappe (42–53)

A22   Robert V. Whitlow

A23   Bob Kennedy

A24   Laraine Day

A25   The Brooklyn Dodgers
The Cincinnati Reds
The St. Louis Cardinals
The New York Yankees

A26   Happy Chandler (Durocher contended that he was banished without
cause.)

A27   Durocher left in the middle of a nationally televised game with the
Dodgers to visit his wife's son at the camp. He told the team he was ill,
but the truth soon came out.

THE SUITS

Q28 Who replaced Cub skipper Leo Durocher halfway through the 1972 season?

Q29 For what team did manager Jim Lefevrbre once serve as a batboy?

Q30 What club did Jim Frey manage before coming to the Cubs in 1984?

Q31 Despite a .302 career batting average, two batting titles, and 14 seasons as a professional ballplayer, Jim Frey never made it to the majors. In what club's farm system did Frey play ball?

Q32 Jim Frey was a major league manager from 1980 through 1981 and again from 1984 through 1986. With what club was he associated in 1982 and 1983?

Q33 On May 15, 1975, Jim Essian was traded to the White Sox for the first of two times during his career. Whose rights did Chicago give up to acquire the catcher?

Q34 Name the minor league club with whom Essian ended his professional career.

THE UNIFORMS

Q1 What do Frank Schulte, Rogers Hornsby, Gabby Hartnett, Phil Cavarretta, Hank Sauer, Ernie Banks, Ryne Sandberg, and Andre Dawson all have in common?

Q2 Jerome Walton captured the NL Rookie of the Year award at the end of the 1989 campaign. What teammate did he edge out for the honor?

Q3 Name the Cub hurler who won the 1990 Rawlings Gold Glove award with 94 chances (39 putouts, 55 assists) and no errors.

Q4 Who was the first NLer to snag back-to-back MVP awards?

Q5 Name the three Cubs who are proud owners of the Cy Young Award.

Q6 Rick Sutcliffe was the fourth NL hurler to win the Cy Young Award unanimously. What other pitchers swept all of the votes?

Q7 Gabby Hartnett became a part of history when he caught Carl Hubbell in the 1934 All-Star Game. Who were the five players Hubbell fanned in succession?

CHICAGO CUBS

A28 Whitey Lockman (Durocher managed the team from 1966 through 1972 and had a 535–526 record.)

A29 The Los Angeles Dodgers

A30 The Kansas City Royals (He led them in 1980 and 1981, winning the pennant in his first term.)

A31 The Baltimore Orioles

A32 The New York Mets (He was their batting coach.)

A33 Dick Allen's (Allen retired after the 1974 season, and Chicago sold his rights to Atlanta for a player to be named later. That player was Essian.)

A34 The Miami Marlins (1985)

–––––––––––––––––––– · ––––––––––––––––––––

A1 Each player has captured the league's MVP award.

A2 Dwight Smith

A3 Greg Maddux

A4 Ernie Banks (1958, 1959)

A5 Ferguson Jenkins (1971)
Bruce Sutter (1979)
Rick Sutcliffe (1984)

A6 Sandy Koufax
Bob Gibson
Steve Carlton

A7 Babe Ruth
Joe Cronin
Lou Gehrig
Jimmie Foxx
Al Simmons

Q8   Who was the first Cub to win a Cy Young Award?

Q9   Identify the North Sider who became the first player in team history to crack three hits in his major league debut.

Q10   Who is the first position player to make four relief-pitching appearances for the Cubs in this century?

Q11   The first National League dinger was an inside-the-park homer on May 2, 1876. Name the Chicago batting star who is credited with the hit.

Q12   The White Stockings revolutionized the game of baseball (and extended a number of careers) in 1880 when they introduced the pitching rotation. Who were the first two pitchers involved in this new concept?

Q13   Charged with playing baseball on the Sabbath, this Cub's acquittal paved the way for Sunday ball games. Name this Chicago player.

Q14   What North Side manager is credited with fielding the famous Tinker-Evers-Chance combination?

Q15   Only three Cubs have recorded three triples in a game since 1900. Name the troika.

Q16   What were the first names of Tinker, Evers, and Chance?

Q17   Tinker, Evers, and Chance appeared together for the first time on September 1, 1902, but they weren't in the SS—2B—1B positions that earned them immortality. What positions did the trio play that day?

Q18   What third baseman shared the diamond with Tinker, Evers, and Chance from 1906 through 1910?

Q19   What was Mordecai Brown's nickname?

Q20   In the "Merkle's Boner" game of 1908, this player retrieved Giant Al Bridwell's single in the outfield and alerted Johnny Evers that Merkle had not touched second base. He then relayed it to Evers for the force-out that ended the game in a tie. Who should be credited with reviving the Cubs' pennant chances?

Q21   Over a four-year period (1906–09), this Cub pitcher's winning percentage never dipped below .750. Who was he?

Q22   On May 2, 1917, the greatest pitching duel in the history of the major leagues took place as two no-hitters were tossed in the same game. Name the Chicago hurler and his Cincinnati counterpart.

CHICAGO CUBS

A8   Ferguson Jenkins (1971)

A9   Doug Dascenzo (1988)

A10   Doug Dascenzo (He pitched in one game in 1990 and three in 1991.)

A11   Ross Barnes (off Cincinnati's William "Cherokee" Fisher)

A12   Larry Corcoran
Fred Goldsmith

A13   Walter Wilmot

A14   Frank Selee

A15   Charlie Hollocher (August 13, 1922)
Ernie Banks (June 11, 1966)
Shawon Dunston (July 28, 1990)

A16   Joe Tinker
Johnny Evers
Frank Chance

A17   Evers—SS
Tinker—3B
Chance—1B
(They played SS–2B–1B for the first time on September 13, 1902.)

A18   Harry Steinfeldt

A19   "Three Finger"

A20   "Circus" Solly Hofman

A21   Mordecai Brown (26–6, 20–6, 29–9, 27–9)

A22   Chicago: Jim "Hippo" Vaughn
Cincinnati: Fred Toney
(Vaughn lost his no-hitter and the game in the 10th inning when Jim
Thorpe, of Olympic fame, hit the game-winning RBI.)

Q23 Pitcher Jim "Hippo" Vaughn stole home plate during a game on August 9, 1919. Who is the only Cub pitcher since to do the same?

Q24 Name the early-day Cub who did the following in a 1927 game against Pittsburgh: He took Paul Waner's liner, stepped on second to double Lloyd Waner, and then tagged Clyde Barnhart coming from first for an unassisted triple play.

Q25 What was Gabby Hartnett's nickname?

Q26 Rogers Hornsby saw action in only 42 games during the 1930 season because of a broken ankle. Who replaced him at second base for most of the year?

Q27 Name the rookie who displaced Rogers Hornsby from second base to third in the 1931 Cub season.

Q28 After being acquired from the Yankees during the 1932 season, this Cub batted .353 in 33 late-season games, but was voted only a half-share of the World Series proceeds by his Chicago teammates. Name this player.

Q29 Player-coach Gabby Hartnett was replaced in the middle of the 1940 season with another catcher. Who was he?

Q30 This Cub second baseman made a less than impressive debut when he committed four errors in the 1941 Opening Day game at Wrigley Field. Who was he?

Q31 After suiting up with the Boston Celtics for two seasons, this first baseman played one game for the 1949 Brooklyn Dodgers and 66 games with the '51 Cubs before heading west for a new career. Name this versatile athlete.

Q32 On May 12, 1955, this Cub pitcher emerged with a 4–0 victory over the Pittsburgh Pirates and completed the first no-hitter by a black pitcher in big league history. Who was he?

Q33 Of the 44 home runs Ernie Banks stroked in 1955, how many were grand slams?

Q34 Who broke Ernie Banks's single-season grand slam record in 1989?

Q35 In what category did Ernie Banks lead the majors in 1955, 1957, 1958, 1959, and 1960?

Q36 In what year was "Mr. Cub" converted to first base?

CHICAGO CUBS

A23   Rick Sutcliffe (On June 29, 1988, he stole home in a game against the Philadelphia Phillies.)

A24   Jim "Scoops" Cooney

A25   "Ol' Tomato Face"

A26   Footsie Blair

A27   Billy Herman

A28   Mark Koenig

A29   Jimmie Wilson

A30   Lou Stringer

A31   Chuck Connors (better known as "The Rifleman")

A32   Sam "Toothpick" Jones

A33   Five (which set a record)

A34   Don Mattingly (with six grand salamis)

A35   Most home runs in a season by a shortstop
(1955: 44; 1957: 43; 1958: 47; 1959: 45; 1960: 41)

A36   1962

***   CUB FAST FACTS   ***

Ferguson Jenkins is the only pitcher in major league history to register more than 3,000 strikeouts while giving up fewer than 1,000 walks. (He gave up 997 bases on balls.) He is also the first Canadian inducted into the Hall of Fame at Cooperstown.

***   CUB FAST FACTS   ***

Adrian "Cap" Anson became the first man to whack more than 3,000 hits in his career. He played for Chicago from 1876 to 1897 and managed the team from 1879 to 1897.

Q37   Ernie Banks's 500th dinger took place at Wrigley Field on May 12, 1970. What Atlanta Brave pitcher gave up the round-tripper?

Q38   Banks's closest rivals for the Cubs' all-time grand slam record are Bill Nicholson and Billy Williams, who are tied with eight. By how many grand slams did Banks outpace them?

Q39   As an instructor in the minors, this Hall of Famer advised the Cubs that Billy Williams belonged in the bigs. Who gave Williams his vote of confidence?

Q40   For how many consecutive seasons did Billy Williams smack 20 or more home runs after making his big league debut in 1959?

Q41   *The Sporting News* selected Williams as the 1972 Major League Player of the Year, but he finished second in the RBI race and NL MVP voting. Who bested him for both these honors?

Q42   One of Williams's many records was consecutive years (nine) with 600 or more at-bats (1962–70). Who surpassed Billy's record?

Q43   Who replaced Williams in left field when his consecutive-game string ended on September 4, 1970?

Q44   On September 3, 1970, Billy Williams asked to be kept out of the lineup, ending his National League record of 1,117 consecutive games played. Who surpassed Williams's mark?

Q45   Williams played his final season as a DH with an American League contender. From what club did Williams retire in 1976?

Q46   What Cub Hall of Famer spent parts of two winters in the late 1960s touring with the Harlem Globetrotters?

Q47   What 1960s-era player was routinely disguised in a hat and coat and positioned in the Wrigley Field bleachers so he could steal signs from opposing pitchers?

Q48   At what college was Don Kessinger All-Conference in both baseball and basketball?

Q49   What Cub second baseman, who won Gold Glove and Rookie of the Year honors, was killed in a plane crash in 1964?

Q50   Who is the only player to make his professional debut with Chicago after the inception of the amateur Free Agent Draft in 1965?

CHICAGO CUBS

A37 Pat Jarvis

A38 Four (Banks had a total of 12 in his tenure with the Cubs.)

A39 Rogers Hornsby

A40 13 (1961–73)

A41 Johnny Bench

A42 Pete Rose

A43 Cleo James

A44 Steve Garvey (L.A. Dodgers, San Diego Padres: 1,207 games)

A45 The Oakland A's

A46 Ferguson Jenkins

A47 Bob Buhl

A48 The University of Mississippi

A49 Ken Hubbs

A50 Burt Hooton (1971)

*** CUB FAST FACTS ***

The Cubs set three NL playoff records in Game 1 of the 1984 NLCS:
Most hits in a game—16
Most home runs in a game—5
Most runs scored in a game—13

*** CUB FAST FACTS ***

Andre Dawson was in good company when he became the second player in the annals of big league baseball to have at least 2,000 hits, 300 homers, and 300 stolen bases. Willie Mays is the only other player to reach all three plateaus.

THE UNIFORMS

Q16 (The Uniforms). What were the first names of Tinker, Evers, and Chance?

CHICAGO CUBS

Q75 (The Uniforms). Off what pitcher did Ryne Sandberg get his first big league hit when he debuted in the majors in 1981?

Q84 (The Uniforms). Rick Sutcliffe achieved this feat on July 29, 1988, and became the first Cub pitcher to do so in sixty-nine years. What did Sutcliffe accomplish?

CHICAGO CUBS

Q1 (Trades, Waives, and Acquisitions). In a 1903 trade that undoubtedly favored Chicago, the Cubs sent Jack Taylor and Harry McLean to the St. Louis Cardinals for Jack O'Neill and this Hall of Famer. Who was he?

Q51   Only two Cubs have had two 100-RBI seasons since 1970. Who are they?

Q52   Name the four Cubs who went to the 1969 All-Star Game.

Q53   The trade that brought Ferguson Jenkins to Chicago from the Phillies in 1966 was a five-player deal. Name the other four players involved in the transaction.

Q54   Within two days of his arrival in Chicago, Jenkins recorded his first Cub win. Name the pitcher he defeated in his debut.

Q55   How many consecutive 20-win seasons did Ferguson Jenkins have with the Cubs?

Q56   Jenkins was enshrined in the Hall of fame in 1991 with Rod Carew and Gaylord Perry. Besides the induction, what does Fergie have in common with Perry and Carew?

Q57   A man who had a brief playing career with the North Siders was enshrined in Cooperstown at the same time as Jenkins. Who is he?

Q58   Jenkins was only the third Cub pitcher to win 20 games in six consecutive seasons (1967–72). Who were the first two?

Q59   Jenkins tied a major league record during the 1967 All-Star Game when he struck out how many batters in three innings?

Q60   Jenkins registered a 20–15 record in 1968. What major league record did he equal that season?

Q61   On May 25, 1982, Jenkins registered the 3,000th strikeout of his career. Who did he fan to reach that plateau?

Q62   Name the four teams that Jenkins played for during his major league career.

Q63   Ferguson Jenkins is one of only five pitchers in the majors to win 100 games in each league. Who are the other four?

Q64   Against what team did Burt Hooton throw a no-hitter at Wrigley Field on April 16, 1972?

Q65   Clay Bryant did it in 1937. Claude Passeau performed the same feat in 1941, as did John Miller in 1947. Twenty-five years elapsed before Burt Hooton managed to duplicate the effort. What did the four pitchers do?

CHICAGO CUBS

A51   Billy Williams (1965: 108; 1970: 129; 1972: 122)
Andre Dawson (1987: 137; 1990: 100)

A52   Ernie Banks
Glenn Beckert
Don Kessinger
Ron Santo

A53   Adolfo Phillips and John Herrnstein came to the Cubs along with Fergie
for pitchers Bob Buhl and Larry Jackson.

A54   Don Sutton (Jenkins homered and drove in both runs in a 2–1 victory
over the Dodgers.)

A55   Six

A56   None of the players appeared in a World Series game.

A57   Joe Garagiola (who was inducted as a member of the media)

A58   Clark Griffith (1894–99)
Mordecai Brown (1906–11)

A59   Six (tying Carl Hubbell's mark: July 10, 1934—three innings)

A60   He had five 1-0 decisions during the year.

A61   Padre Gary Templeton (in San Diego)

A62   Philadelphia (1965–66)
Cubs (1966–73; 1982–83)
Texas (1974–75; 1978–81)
Boston (1976–77)

A63   Cy Young
Jim Bunning
Gaylord Perry
Nolan Ryan

A64   The Philadelphia Phillies (4–0)

A65   Each of them hit a grand slam.

Q66 On September 2, 1972, this Cub pitcher beat the Padres, 8–0, and missed a perfect game when he walked Larry Stahl on a 3-2 pitch with two out in the ninth. Name the hurler who fell just short of perfection.

Q67 Who was called the Brooks Robinson of the National League?

Q68 In the 1975 All-Star Game, this Cub batting king hammered a game-winning, bases-loaded single in the ninth inning to snap a 3–3 deadlock and propel the NL to a 6–3 win in Milwaukee. Name him.

Q69 On April 25, 1976, at Dodger Stadium, this North Sider saved the American flag from being set on fire by two protesters in the outfield. Who earned the label "Mr. Red, White, and Blue"?

Q70 This player hit three home runs in a game twice in his career—once while playing for Chicago and the other while playing against the Cubs. Who is he?

Q71 Name the two Cub switch-hitters who homered from both sides of the plate in one season during the 1980s (1981–90).

Q72 Who were the only two Cub pitchers to record triples in the 1980s?

Q73 This Sox coach had a career-best game as a player while catching for the Cubs. On April 22, 1980, he collected eight RBIs and a game-winning grand slam to lead Chicago over the Cardinals at Wrigley Field. Who is he?

Q74 Who was named Minor League Player of the Year by *Baseball America* after he compiled a 19–3 record at Hawaii in 1984?

Q75 Off what pitcher did Ryne Sandberg get his first big league hit when he debuted in the majors in 1981?

Q76 Ryne Sandberg had a strong rookie season at third base when he joined the Cubbies in 1982. Why was he switched to second base one year later?

Q77 Ryne Sandberg had consecutive 30-homer seasons in 1989 and 1990. How many second basemen in major league history have hit the 30-or-more mark in back-to-back years?

Q78 Ryne Sandberg is one of the three big league players to hit 40 homers and steal 25 bases in the same season. Name the other two.

Q79 Only two second basemen have hit more home runs in a season than Ryne Sandberg, who stroked 40 taters in 1990. Who is ahead of Ryno in the dinger derby?

CHICAGO CUBS

A66   Milt Pappas

A67   Ron Santo (for his fielding abilities)

A68   Bill Madlock

A69   Rick Monday

A70   Dave Kingman

A71   Bump Wills (1982)
Damon Berryhill (1988)

A72   Ferguson Jenkins (September 3, 1983)
Rick Sutcliffe (August 23, 1987)

A73   Barry Foote

A74   Mike Bielecki

A75   Cub Mike Krukow at Wrigley Field

A76   Ron Cey was inserted at the hot corner, so Sandberg was moved to second base.

A77   None—Sandberg is the first. (1989: 30; 1990: 40)

A78   Hank Aaron (1968: 29 homers, 28 stolen bases)
José Canseco (1988: 42 dingers, 40 thefts)

A79   Davey Johnson of Atlanta; 43 HRs in 1973
Rogers Hornsby of St. Louis; 42 HRs in 1922

*** CUB FAST FACTS ***

The Maddux brothers—Greg of Chicago and Mike of the Phillies—made big league history when they faced each other in a September 1986 game. Greg emerged victorious in the first match of rookie brothers in the majors.

*** CUB FAST FACTS ***

Not a single home run was hit in the six-game 1918 Cub-Red Sox World Series.

Q80 On September 8, 1985, Pete Rose singled at Wrigley to equal Ty Cobb's record for most hits in major league history. Name the Chicago pitcher who gave up the hit.

Q81 Name the Cub who was tied for the most losses (17) in the AL during the 1986 season.

Q82 When Greg Maddux made his major league pitching debut on September 2, 1986, he was the youngest Cub to see action in 19 years. Who was younger when he started for Chicago?

Q83 Angered with the trade that sent them to the Texas Rangers, Rafael Palmeiro and Jamie Moyer expressed their displeasure with custom-made T-shirts. What did the message say?

Q84 Rick Sutcliffe achieved this feat on July 29, 1988, and became the first Cub pitcher to do so in 69 years. What did Sutcliffe accomplish?

Q85 Leonard "King" Cole threw a shutout for the Cubs in his major league debut in 1909. It took 79 years before another Cub duplicated that effort. Name the pitcher who achieved the same feat in 1988.

Q86 Danny Jackson finished second in the balloting for the National League's 1988 Cy Young Award. Who won the honor that season?

Q87 In 1989, Joe Girardi was the first rookie catcher to start on Opening Day for the Cubs in over two decades. Who was the last first-year catcher before Girardi to start in the season opener?

Q88 Name the Cub crooner who sang the national anthem on two occasions: in July 1989 and at the 1991 home opener at Wrigley.

Q89 When 36-year-old André Dawson hit the 100-RBI mark in 1990, he became the second-oldest Cub in this century to reach that plateau. What player was two years older than the Hawk when he drove in 106 runs in 1969?

Q90 Age was no hindrance for 36-year-old Andre Dawson as he hit .310 and, for the third time in his career, knocked in 100 runs during the 1990 season. Who was the only other Cub since 1970 to amass 100-plus RBIs more than once?

Q91 Who led the National League in blown saves for the 1990 season?

Q92 In 1945, Phil Cavarretta, Stan Hack, and Don Johnson each finished the season with .300-plus batting averages. Forty-five years later, another Cub trio reached that plateau. Name the sluggers.

CHICAGO CUBS

A80 Reggie Patterson

A81 Richard Dotson (He was tied with Baltimore's Mike Morgan.)

A82 Rick James (1967: 19 years old)

A83 "I got Frey-ed and Zimmered."

A84 He stole home.

A85 Jeff Pico (May 31, 1988; 4–0 over Cincinnati)

A86 Orel Hershiser

A87 Randy Hundley (1966)

A88 Dwight Smith

A89 Ernie Banks

A90 Billy Williams (1970 and 1972)

A91 Paul Assenmacher

A92 Andre Dawson (.310)
Mark Grace (.309)
Ryne Sandberg (.306)

*** CUB FAST FACTS ***

The year 1990 was a memorable one for Ryne Sandberg, as he became the first second baseman in big league history to reach the 30-HR mark in consecutive seasons and the first player in history to have both a 40-homer season and a 50-steal season during his career.

*** CUB FAST FACTS ***

George Bell's Legacy With the Cubs
Contract—$9.8 million guaranteed over three years
Batting Average—.285
Home Runs—25
RBIs—86
Season With the Cubs—1 (1991)

THE UNIFORMS

Q93   Name the Cub who was tops in the All-Star balloting for two consecutive years: 1990 and 1991.

Q94   When Danny Jackson pitched on April 9, 1991, he became only the second southpaw to throw on Opening Day for the team. Who was the first lefty to open for the team?

Q95   The Cubs featured three former MVPs on their 1991 roster. Name the players and the teams for whom they played when they received the honor.

Q96   It wasn't until June 14, 1991, that Danny Jackson registered his first Cub victory, after six starts and two losses. Against what club did he get his first win?

Q97   For what three teams has Danny Jackson had the honor of being the Opening Day pitcher?

Q98   Besides wearing the same uniform number (24), what do Chico Walker and Willie Mays have in common?

Q99   This Cub's middle name is Kealoha, which means "Loved One" in Hawaiian. Who is he?

Q100 A converted shortstop, this pitcher had to change positions because he couldn't hit well enough. He came to the Cubs in 1992 and promptly hit a home run in his first at-bat in Chicago. Name this player.

SETTING THE STANDARD

Q1   On July 13, 1877, Chicago's George Bradley stepped aside to allow teammate Cal McVey to pitch a game. How many consecutive games had Bradley pitched before that day to establish the all-time record?

Q2   When Don Cardwell took the mound on May 15, 1960, he did something no other pitcher in big league history had done in his first appearance with a team. What did Cardwell do?

Q3   Who established a Cub single-season record for saves by a southpaw, with 36 in his debut season with the team?

Q4   Who set a Cub record for relievers by throwing 30.2 consecutive scoreless innings.

CHICAGO CUBS

A93   Ryne Sandberg

A94   Dick Ellsworth (1965)

A95   George Bell (1987: Toronto)
Andre Dawson (1987: Montreal)
Ryne Sandberg (1984: Chicago)

A96   The Padres, at San Diego

A97   The Chicago Cubs (1991)
The Cincinnati Reds (1989)
The Kansas City Royals (1987)

A98   They are the only players to belt inside-the-park grand slams in Candlestick Park. (Mays: 1960; Walker: 1991)

A99   Shawn Boskie

A100   Jim Bullinger

A1   88 consecutive games (The record still stands.)

A2   He threw a no-hitter in his debut appearance for the Cubs.

A3   Mitch Williams (36 of 47 in 1989)

A4   Les Lancaster (In 1989, he did not allow a run until his 21st appearance.)

*** CUB FAST FACTS ***

Bill Madlock was the first player in major league history to win a pair of batting crowns with two different teams: the Cubs (1975 and 1976) and Pittsburgh (1981 and 1983). He was also the only right-handed batter to lead the National League in batting average between 1971 and 1989.

SETTING THE STANDARD

Q5 Name the Cub who equaled a major league record by striking out four batters in one inning.

Q6 The Cubs' dismal streak of nine consecutive defeats in 1991 was not a club mark. What is the team's record for straight losses?

Q7 Wilson Alvarez threw a no-hitter in his second major league appearance. Who is the only player to toss a no-no in his first game in the bigs?

Q8 Name the early-day Cub who was called into a 1915 game against the Brooklyn Dodgers with two outs in the first inning, won 4–3 in 19 innings, and thus recorded the longest relief effort ever in the big leagues.

Q9 Name the two Cubs who have hitting streaks of 30 or more games.

Q10 Among Jerome Walton's achievements in his stellar 1989 rookie year was his 30-game hitting streak (.338; July 21–August 20). Whose modern-day team record did he shatter by two games?

Q11 What Cub equaled a modern major league record by belting three triples in a game?

Q12 Who was the first Cub to belt 150 dingers and steal 150 bases?

Q13 Babe Ruth established a major league record in 1919 when he hit 29 home runs during the season. Name the Chicago player who held the record before the Bambino.

Q14 This player whacked 56 home runs during the 1930 season and set a team and NL record in the process. Who was wielding the hot bat?

Q15 George Bell's 28 homers on the road in 1987 tied an AL standard set in the early 1960s. Whose record did Bell match?

Q16 Only three Cub shortstops have ever hit 17 or more homers in a season. Who are they?

Q17 Heinie Zimmerman set a Cub record in 1911 that stands to this day. What did Zimmerman do in the June 11, 1911, game against the Boston Braves?

Q18 Name the only North Sider who has had five RBIs in one inning.

Q19 The Phillies' Juan Samuel broke the major league mark for rookies in 1984 when he registered 701 at-bats. Name the Cub whose record he shattered.

CHICAGO CUBS

A5   Paul Assenmacher (August 22, 1989; while pitching for the Braves. One hitter reached base on a wild pitch on a called third strike.)

A6   13 (1985)

A7   Bobo Holloman (of the St. Louis Browns; May 6, 1953)

A8   George "Zip" Zabel

A9   Bill Dahlen (1894: 42 games)
Jerome Walton (1989: 30 games)

A10   Ron Santo's

A11   Shawon Dunston (July 28, 1990; at Montreal)

A12   Ryne Sandberg

A13   Ned Williamson (1884: 27 homers)

A14   Lewis "Hack" Wilson

A15   Harmon Killebrew's

A16   Roy Smalley (1950: 21 HRs)
Ernie Banks (1954 through 1961)
Shawon Dunston (1990: 17 HRs)

A17   Zimmerman racked up nine RBIs in the game.

A18   Billy Williams (On May 1, 1964, Williams hit a grand slam and had a run-scoring single in Chicago's 11 3 drubbing of Houston.)

*** CUB FAST FACTS ***

MR. CUB—ERNIE BANKS
From 1955 to 1960, Ernie Banks hit more homers than anyone in the majors (including Mickey Mantle, Willie Mays, and Hank Aaron). An 11-time All-Star, he was NL MVP twice, led the league twice in home runs and RBIs, and was the first Cub to have his number retired.

Q20 What Chicago player set an early-day record for steals in a game, with seven?

Q21 This early-day Cub performed a feat in 1915 that no one on the team has been able to duplicate since then. What did Wilson Good do in an August 18, 1915, game against Brooklyn?

Q22 What North Sider became the first National Leaguer to play 1,000 consecutive games?

Q23 Andre Dawson is one of two players in major league history with at least 2,000 hits, 300 homers, and 300 stolen bases. Who is the other?

Q24 In a 1990 game, Andre Dawson set a big league record for intentional walks in a single contest. How many did the Hawk receive?

Q25 On July 12, 1991, Doug Dascenzo established a fielding record when he made his 227th straight appearance in the outfield without an error. Whose NL record did Dascenzo top?

Q26 How many consecutive appearances did Doug Dascenzo make in the Cubs' outfield before he committed his first big league error in a 1991 game against the Padres?

FYI

Q1 How did the Cubs get their nickname?

Q2 In the late 1800s, the term "Chicagoed" was a part of baseball vernacular. What did the term signify?

Q3 What other city was represented by a team dubbed the "White Stockings" at the same time the Cubs were using the nickname for their club in the late 1800s?

Q4 In a July 1875 game against Chicago, the Phillies Joseph E. Borden made major league history. What did he do?

Q5 True or false. Of the eight original 1876 charter members of the National League, the Cubs are the only team to have operated continuously in the same city.

CHICAGO CUBS

A19 Ken Hubbs (1962: 661 at-bats)

A20 George Gore (June 25, 1881)

A21 He stole second base, third base, and home plate in the same inning.

A22 Billy Williams (He reached that plateau on April 30, 1970.)

A23 Willie Mays

A24 Five (May 22, 1990; vs. Cincinnati)

A25 Curt Flood's (When he set the mark, Dascenzo had handled 421 chances. Flood handled 566 chances.)

A26 242 consecutive appearances (In setting an NL record, Dascenzo handled 442 chances in that time span.)

A1 The team was christened the Cubs because of the number of young players on the roster. (Previously, they were called the "Colts" and the "Orphans." They officially adopted "Cubs" in 1907.)

A2 A shutout. (The White Stockings, the predecessor of the Cubs, was the first team ever to be held scoreless in big-time baseball. The *New York Herald* coined the phrase after a 9–0 Chicago loss to the New York Mutuals on July 23, 1869.)

A3 Philadelphia (The club later changed its name to the Phillies.)

A4 He pitched the first no-hitter.

A5 True (The other charter members: Cincinnati, New York, St. Louis, Louisville, Boston, Philadelphia, and Hartford)

Q6 The Cubs captured the pennant in four of the five years between 1906 and 1910. Who edged out the North Siders in 1909 even though they won 104 games?

Q7 The Cubs were the first National League club to break the million-fan plateau at the turnstiles. In what year was the record set?

Q8 The Cubs played in five different facilities before they landed at Wrigley Field in 1916. Name the ballparks.

Q9 Who is Zachary Taylor Davis?

Q10 Wrigley Field was originally named Weegman Park. What baseball team was the first to play in the facility?

Q11 True or false. Only two players have ever hit the center field scoreboard in Wrigley Field.

Q12 Wrigley Field, the third-oldest ballpark in the major leagues, was built in 1914. Which cities have older stadiums?

Q13 Though modified, the Wrigley scoreboard has remained intact since it was originally erected. In what year was the scoreboard constructed?

Q14 Who was the Cubs' first Opening Day pitcher when the team debuted at Wrigley Field in 1916?

Q15 What three names has Wrigley Field had since it was built in 1914?

Q16 The first National League game played at Wrigley took place on April 20, 1916. Who did the Cubs defeat that day, 7–6, in 11 innings?

Q17 It was 47 years before the first night game at Wrigley and P. K. Wrigley ordered the light towers and bulbs up so the Cubs could play home night games. What prevented the lights from going up in the stadium?

Q18 Who did the Cubs play on August 9, 1988, in the first Wrigley Field (complete) night game?

Q19 Who was the Cubs' starting pitcher on August 9, 1988, the first official night game in Wrigley Field history?

Q20 How many times has the All-Star Game been held at Wrigley Field?

Q21 The Cubs are one of two big league teams permitted to hold day-night doubleheaders. What other team is allowed to do so?

CHICAGO CUBS

A6   The Pittsburgh Pirates

A7   1927 (1,163,347 fans)

A8   23rd Street Grounds (1876–77)
Lakefront Park (1878–84)
West Side Park (1885–92)
West Side Grounds (1893–1915)
South Side Park (1891–94; games split between West Side and South Side parks)

A9   The architect who designed Wrigley Field and old Comiskey Park

A10   The Chicago Whales (1914–15; of the Federal League)

A11   False—no one has ever hit the board, although Roberto Clemente and Bill Nicholson came close by hitting homers to left-center field and right-center field, respectively.)

A12   Detroit (Tiger Stadium; built in 1900)
Boston (Fenway Park; built in 1912)

A13   1937

A14   Claude Hendrix (Cubs 7, Reds 6, in 11 innings)

A15   Weegman Park (1914–20)
Cubs Park (1920–26)
Wrigley Field (1926–   )

A16   The Cincinnati Reds

A17   World War II (Wrigley donated the steel for the lighting equipment to the war effort after Pearl Harbor was bombed, thus delaying the Cubs' first night game until August 9, 1988.)

A18   The New York Mets (The Cubs triumphed, 6–4.)

A19   Mike Bielecki

A20   Three times (1947, 1962, 1990)

A21   The Boston Red Sox (because of Fenway's small capacity—33,461)

Q22 The 1991 Cubs were the fifth club in baseball history to feature three former MVPs on their roster. Name the other teams.

Q23 WGN-TV analyst Steve Stone is a Cy Young Award winner. For whom was he pitching when he earned the honor?

Q24 Harry Caray joined the Cub broadcast team in 1982. For what three teams did he broadcast before the Cubs?

Q25 Why was the Cubs' 5–3 loss to the Atlanta Braves early in the 1991 season significant in the annals of broadcast history?

GLORY DAYS

Q1 The Cubs' top hitter in the 1906 Series was a player who appeared in only 64 games during the regular season. Name the center fielder who played in every inning of the Series and batted .304.

Q2 Who threw a one-hitter in Game 2 of the 1906 Series?

Q3 Game 1 of the 1907 Series saw Detroit winning 3–2 with two outs in the ninth. The Tigers got the third out, but a dropped ball on the third strike allowed the batter to take first and the tying run to score. Who was at bat on the play?

Q4 In the above play, what Tiger catcher allowed Chicago to tie the game?

Q5 After the first game of the 1907 Series ended in a tie (due to darkness), the Cubbies swept Detroit in four straight. Of the 48 innings played, how many scoreless innings did Chicago pitchers toss?

Q6 The game known for "Merkle's Boner" propelled the Cubs into the 1908 playoffs, though it took place a month before the end of the season. What was "Merkle's Boner"?

Q7 Of the 10 games played in the 1907 and 1908 World Series (including one tie), Detroit was victorious in one game. Who was the Detroit ace responsible for the lone win?

Q8 In 1908, the Cubs again met the Tigers in the Series. For the second year in a row, Game 1 saw Detroit leading 6–5 in the ninth inning, only to fritter away the victory. Whose bases-loaded single propelled Chicago to a 10–6 win?

CHICAGO CUBS

A22   The New York Yankees (1961, 1964)
The Cincinnati Reds (1964, 1976, 1978)
The Boston Red Sox (1979)
The California Angels (1982)

A23   The Baltimore Orioles (1980)

A24   The St. Louis Cardinals (1945–69)
The Oakland A's (1970)
The White Sox (1971–81)

A25   It was the first time three generations of a family—Harry, Skip, and Chip Caray—called the same major league game.

———————————— . ————————————

A1   "Circus" Solly Hofman

A2   Ed Reulbach

A3   Del Howard (who was batting for Joe Tinker)

A4   Charlie Schmidt

A5   43

A6   After an apparent game-winning base hit, Giant Fred Merkle, the runner on first base, did not advance to second. When he saw the winning run cross home plate, he turned and ran off the field. As fans raced onto the field to celebrate, Johnny Evers got the ball and touched second base for a force-out. The fans stormed the field, and the game ended in a tie. It was replayed at the end of the season, with the Cubs and Giants tied for the pennant. Chicago won the game and went into the 1908 Series.

A7   George Mullin

A8   Solly Hofman (off Tiger pitcher Ed Summers)

GLORY DAYS

Q9 What Cub regular missed the 1910 World Series due to a broken ankle?

Q10 The Cubs lost the 1910 Series in five games to the Philadelphia Athletics. Identify the only Chicago pitcher to win a game.

Q11 Why wasn't the 1918 Series between Chicago and Boston truly a "fall classic"?

Q12 Neither Chicago nor Boston had a "home field" advantage in the 1918 Series, since both clubs opted to play away from their regular-season fields. In what two parks was the Series played that year?

Q13 What Red Sox pitcher established a Series record in the 1918 fall classic when he tossed his 29th consecutive scoreless postseason inning during Game 4?

Q14 The greatest reversal in Series history took place in the seventh inning of Game 4 in 1929. How many runs did the Philadelphia Athletics score to overcome an 8–0 Chicago lead?

Q15 What former Chicago manager led the New York Yankees against the Cubs in the 1932 World Series?

Q16 Legend has it that Babe Ruth pointed to the right field bleachers in Wrigley Field and promptly belted a homer to that spot in the 1932 World Series. What Chicago battery was on the field for the historic play?

Q17 Game 6 of the 1935 World Series was tied 3–3 in the top of the ninth inning. The Cubs had a great opportunity to score when they placed a man on third base without an out, but they failed to bring him home. Who was stranded on the hot corner?

Q18 Name the three Cubs who failed to drive in the go-ahead run in the ninth inning of the sixth game of the 1935 Series.

Q19 It was Gabby Hartnett's home run with two out, an 0-2 count, and the game against the Pirates about to be called due to darkness that propelled the Cubs into the 1938 World Series. Name the Pittsburgh pitcher who gave up the decisive dinger.

Q20 Acquired on waivers from the Yankees in July 1945, this pitcher won 11 of 13 decisions for the Cubs to lead them to the 1945 NL pennant. In the Series, he pitched in four games and 18 innings, posting a 2–2 record. Name him.

Q21 What Cub ace tossed a one-hitter in Game 3 of the 1945 World Series, and who ruined his no-hitter?

CHICAGO CUBS

A9 Johnny Evers

A10 Mordecai Brown (In the fourth game, he came in to relieve Leonard "King" Cole in the eighth inning and pitched two innings in Chicago's 4–3 win.)

A11 The Series was moved to late summer—September 5 to 11—in compliance with a federal government edict prompted by the United States's entry into World War I.

A12 Chicago: Comiskey Park (rather than Weegman Park)
Boston: Braves Field (rather than Fenway Park)
(The clubs chose the alternate sites because of their larger seating capacity.)

A13 Babe Ruth (The string of scoreless innings started during the 1916 Series.)

A14 10

A15 Joe McCarthy

A16 Pitcher: Charlie Root
Catcher: Gabby Hartnett

A17 Stan Hack (The Tigers scored in the bottom of the inning to win the game, 4–3, and the Series, 4–2.)

A18 Billy Jurges (struck out)
Larry French (grounded back to the pitcher's mound)
Augie Galan (flew out)

A19 Mace Brown (The Cubs clinched the pennant two days later, on September 30.)

A20 Hank Borowy

A21 Claude Passeau was on the hill.
Rudy York singled in the second inning.

Q22   With the score knotted 7–7, Game 6 of the 1945 Series went into extra innings. Who hit a ground-rule double to knock in the winning run?

Q23   What base runner scored the winning run for Chicago in Game 6 of the 1945 Series?

Q24   Name the three players who were on both of the Cubs' division-winning teams during the 1980s.

Q25   What Cub set a major league record during the 1984 NL Championship Series when he stroked his fourth consecutive home run in as many games?

Q26   By how many games did the Cubs win their division in 1984, the first title the club had captured since 1945?

Q27   Who tagged Greg Maddux for a grand slam homer in Game 1 of the 1989 National League Championship Series at Wrigley Field?

Q28   Whose home run in the bottom of the ninth inning of Game 4 of the 1984 NL Championship Series won it for San Diego?

Q29   Chicago lost the lead in Game 5 of the 1984 NL Championship Series because of an error in the seventh inning. Who allowed a grounder to go through his legs and the Padres to tie the score, 3–3?

Q30   Name the Chicago slugger who batted .647, had 11 hits, and racked up 19 total bases in the 1989 NL Championship Series, but was overshadowed by the stellar performance of the Giants' "Will the Thrill" Clark.

Q31   The losing pitcher in Game 3 gave up a two-run homer in the seventh inning when he thought the count was 3–0. (It was actually 2–0.) Whose fastball was sent over the left-field fence by Bobby Thompson?

Q32   The Cubs jumped to a one-run lead in Game 5 of the 1989 NL Championship Series when a dropped ball resulted in a man advancing to first. Who wound up on base because of the error?

Q33   In the question cited above, what Giant outfielder dropped the ball in the third inning?

Q34   The Cubs had a chance to extend the '89 NL Championship Series in the ninth inning of Game 5 when they put together three successive two-out singles to get one run back and make the score 3–2. What Chicago player grounded out to end the game and the season for the North Siders?

CHICAGO CUBS

A22   Stan Hack

A23   Billy Schuster (pinch-running for Frank Secory)

A24   Rick Sutcliffe
Ryne Sandberg
Scott Sanderson

A25   Gary Matthews

A26   Six and a half games

A27   Will Clark

A28   Steve Garvey (off Lee Smith)

A29   Leon Durham (off a hit by pinch hitter Tim Flannery)

A30   Mark Grace (In the five-game series, Clark batted .650, stroked 13 hits, and had 24 total bases.)

A31   Les Lancaster's

A32   Jerome Walton

A33   Kevin Mitchell

A34   Ryne Sandberg

*** CUB FAST FACTS ***

On August 5, 1975, Bill Bonham (1971–77) set a major league record when he allowed seven consecutive hits (three singles, two doubles, and two homers) to start a game.

TRADES, WAIVES, AND ACQUISITIONS

Q1   In a 1903 trade that turned out to be a great one for Chicago, the Cubs send Jack Taylor and Larry McLean to the St. Louis Cardinals for Jack O'Neill and this Hall of Famer. Who was he?

Q2   The Cubs obtained Grover Alexander and Bill Killefer for Mike Prendergast, Pickles Dillhoefer, and $55,000 in a December 1917 deal. With what team did Chicago do business?

Q3   Who came to the North Siders in exchange for Sparky Adams and Pete Scott in a 1927 transaction with the Pirates?

Q4   Five players and $200,000—that was the price William Wrigley, Jr., paid for Rogers Hornsby in 1928. Name the quintet sent to the Boston Braves in the deal.

Q5   How did the Cubs acquire pitcher Burleigh Grimes on the last day of 1931?

Q6   A trade that wasn't fondly remembered saw Dolf Camilli shipped to the Phillies. Who came to the Cubs in this deal during the summer of 1934?

Q7   After the 1938 season, the Cubs sent Bill Jurges and Joe Demaree to the New York Giants for three players. Name the new Cubs.

Q8   Though his career was in its twilight, Dizzy Dean was acquired by Philip Wrigley in 1938 for $185,000 and three players. Name the Cubbies given up in the deal.

Q9   The Cubs virtually gave away Billy Herman when they traded him to the Dodgers on May 6, 1941. What did the club get in return?

Q10   In 1964, the Cubs traded for Ernie Broglio, Bobby Shantz, and Doug Clemens. What Hall of Famer did they give up in what is considered one of the most lopsided deals in baseball history?

Q11   What pitcher did the Cubs unload for Lee Thomas in a 1966 deal with the Atlanta Braves?

Q12   In 1969, the Cubs acquired Nate Oliver from the Yankees for an infielder who would later manage the North Siders for two seasons. Name him.

CHICAGO CUBS

A1   Mordecai Brown

A2   The Philadelphia Phillies

A3   Kiki Cuyler

A4   Lou Legett
Percy Jones
Freddie Maguire
Socks Seibold
Bruce Cunningham

A5   The team traded Hack Williams and Bud Teachout to St. Louis for the services of Grimes.

A6   Don Hurst

A7   Dick Bartell
Hank Leiber
Gus Mancuso

A8   Curt Davis
Clyde Shoun
Tuck Stainback

A9   Johnny Hudson, Charlie Gilbert, and $65,000 (Hudson played only 50 games of the 1941 season, and Gilbert played parts of four seasons with Chicago.)

A10   Lou Brock (along with Paul Toth and Jack Spring)

A11   Ted Abernathy

A12   Lee Elia

*** CUB FAST FACTS ***

Leo Durocher is the only National League manager to pilot two teams in the same season—and he did it twice:
1948—Brooklyn Dodgers and New York Giants
1972—Chicago and Houston Astros

TRADES, WAIVES, AND ACQUISITIONS

Q13 How did Chicago acquire the services of Joe Pepitone in the summer of 1970?

Q14 What backstop did the Cubs trade to the San Diego Padres in exchange for Garry Jestadt in a 1971 swap?

Q15 What Cub pitcher was sent to the Oakland A's for Rick Monday in a 1971 trade?

Q16 In a two-for-one deal, hurlers Geoff Zahn and Eddie Solomon came to the North Siders for a pitcher. Who went to the City of Angels in return in the 1975 deal?

Q17 Who was traded to St. Louis in 1975 for Mike Garman and Bob Hrapmann?

Q18 Who did the Cubs give up for Ken Holtzman in a 1978 deal with the Yankees?

Q19 What club originally signed George Bell as a nondrafted free agent in 1978?

Q20 In a pitcher-for-catcher deal, Chicago acquired Jay Howell from the Reds for this backstop. Name the catcher who went to Cincinnati early in the 1980 campaign.

Q21 From what team did the Cubs purchase Mark Lemongello in 1980?

Q22 In a 1981 swap of outfielders, the Cubs sent Jim Tracy to the Astros. Who came to Chicagoland in return?

Q23 The Cubs traded two players to be named later to the Yankees for Pat Tabler in 1981. Name the pair of players.

Q24 In a swap of shortstops, the Cubs sent Larry Bowa to the Phillies in exchange for Ivan DeJesus. What other player came to the Cubs in the 1982 deal?

Q25 It was a "pitcher perfect" deal, especially for the Cubs, when they acquired Mike Bielecki from Pittsburgh in a 1988 transaction. What hurler did they send to the Steel City in return?

CHICAGO CUBS

A13   Pepitone was purchased from the Houston Astros.

A14   Chris Cannizzaro

A15   Ken Holtzman

A16   Burt Hooton

A17   Don Kessinger

A18   Ron Davis

A19   The Philadelphia Phillies

A20   Mike O'Berry

A21   The Toronto Blue Jays

A22   Gary Woods

A23   Bill Caudill (April 1, 1982)
Jay Howell (August 2, 1982)

A24   Ryne Sandberg

A25   Mike Curtis

***   CUB FAST FACTS   ***

Between the morning and afternoon games of a 1922 Memorial Day doubleheader, Max Flack of the Chicago Cubs was traded to the St. Louis Cardinals for Cliff Heathcote. Both wound up playing one game for each team.

TRADES, WAIVES, AND ACQUISITIONS

Q26   A minor league battery—pitcher Pat Gomez and catcher Kelly Mann—was traded by the Cubs to Atlanta in August 1989. Name the pitcher who was dealt to the North Siders in return.

Q27   Who did Chicago obtain when it sent Greg Smith to the Dodgers on December 14, 1990?

Q28   Who did the Cubs receive as compensation when the Dodgers claimed left-handed pitcher Steve Wilson on waivers in September 1991?

Q29   The Cubs acquired Chuck McElroy and Bob Scanlan from the Phillies in a deal made just prior to the 1981 opener. Who did the Cubbies dispatch to Philly?

Q30   With six games left in the 1991 season, the Cubs traded Damon Berryhill and Mike Bielecki to the Atlanta Braves for a minor league pitching tandem. Steven Wendell was dispatched to winter ball. Who was the other pitcher acquired in the deal?

Q31   This 1992 crosstown trade involved a pair of Dominican outfielders who hailed from the same hometown. Name the former and new Cubs involved in the deal.

CHICAGO CUBS

A26 Paul Assenmacher

A27 José Vizcaino

A28 Right-hander Jeff Hartsock

A29 Mitch Williams

A30 Yorkie Perez (brother of Melido and Pascual)

A31 George Bell went to the White Sox for Sammy Sosa (and reliever Ken Patterson). Both Bell and Sosa hail from San Pedro de Macorís, Dominican Republic.

*** CUB FAST FACTS ***

On July 4, 1966, Ron Santo established a Cub record by hitting in his 28th straight game, but Chicago fell to the Pirates. In the second game of the twin bill, Santo went hitless, and the North Siders won.

Chicago White Sox

CHICAGO WHITE SOX

Chicago White Sox—1919.

THE SUITS

Q1 Which Sox manager has the best regular-season win-loss percentage?

Q2 Name the Sox manager who led the club to more victories in the course of his career than any other manager.

Q3 Among Sox managers with a minimum of 100 games, which has the worst win-loss record?

Q4 Three Sox managers have had two tenures each at the club's helm. Name the trio.

Q5 Who holds the club record for the longest tenure as Sox manager?

Q6 The White Sox have won five pennants and a division crown under a half-dozen different managers. Name the six skippers.

Q7 Who is the only manager in AL history to win a pennant after managing a different team earlier in the season?

Q8 Charles Comiskey was a player-manager for the St. Louis Browns of the American Association in the late 1800s. What innovation did the first baseman bring to the game?

Q9 What club did Charles Comiskey first own?

Q10 In an attempt to revive his club and eradicate the Black Sox stigma, Charles Comiskey revamped a major portion of his team. From what city did he purchase an entire starting infield?

Q11 Manager Fielder Jones (1904–08) improved the game of baseball with two innovations. What were they?

CHICAGO WHITE SOX

A1 Clark Griffith (1901–02: 157–113, .581)

A2 Jimmy Dykes (1935–46: 899 wins)

A3 Lew Fonseca (1932–34: 120–196, .377)

A4 Nixie Callahan (1903–04, 1912–14)
Paul Richards (1951–54, 1978)
Al Lopez (1957–65, 1968–69)

A5 Jimmy Dykes (12 years: 1935–46)

A6 1901: Clark Griffith   1919: Kid Gleason
1906: Fielder Jones   1959: Al Lopez
1917: Clarence Rowland   1983: Tony LaRussa

A7 Bob Lemon (He started the 1978 season with the Sox, left the club on June 30, 1978, and managed the Yankees from late July through the World Series.)

A8 Comiskey was the first man to play away from the base.

A9 Sioux City (of the Western League. He moved the club to St. Paul and called his team the Saints.)

A10 Salt Lake City (of the Pacific Coast League)

A11 The "motion infield" and "body twist" slide

*** SOX FAST FACTS ***

CAREER BATTING LEADERS
Games—Luke Appling (2,422)
Average—Joe Jackson (.339)
Runs—Luke Appling (1,319)
Hits—Luke Appling (2,749)
RBIs—Luke Appling (1,116)
Pinch Hits—Jerry Hairston (87)
Walks—Luke Appling (1,302)
Total Bases—Luke Appling (3,528)
Strikeouts—Harold Baines (782)
Slugging Pct. (1,500 ABs)—Zeke Bonura (.518)
Home Runs—Carlton Fisk (still active as of 1992)

Q12 Fielder Jones's teams were built on pitching, defense, and speed—a radical change from the usual slugging clubs of the day. By what nickname was his club known?

Q13 What general manager caused the White Sox to be evicted from the American League in 1945?

Q14 Name the two big league teams Bill Veeck owned before he took over the helm of the White Sox.

Q15 Always an innovator, Bill Veeck signed the American League's first black player and the league's oldest rookie. Name the pair of players.

Q16 There was a lot of small talk in 1951 when Bill Veeck made Eddie Gaedel a part of baseball folklore. Who was Gaedel?

Q17 In what year did Veeck first purchase a majority share of the Sox?

Q18 On June 10, 1961, Veeck sold his interest in the Sox to his former partner, Arthur Allyn, Jr. What was the name of the corporation under which the Pale Hose were placed?

Q19 Several years ago, Veeck went out on a limb when he donated to a charity auction an item that was once near and dear to him. What did he give?

Q20 Veeck's second tenure as Sox owner started in 1975 when he wrested the sale of the club from Seattle investors. From whom did he purchase the team?

Q21 In 1980, Veeck attempted to sell the Sox to an Ohio businessman, but the league denied the sale because of the prospective owner's racing holdings. Who almost became the new owner of the Chicago franchise?

Q22 After four seasons at the Sox helm (1951–54), Paul Richards resigned to accept the managerial position with another team. Where did Richards go?

Q23 With what team did future Chisox manager Al Lopez capture the AL Championship in 1954?

Q24 Al Lopez is one of the two managers to win an American League pennant during the 1950s. Who is the other?

Q25 Eddie Stanky managed the Sox for two and a half seasons (1966–68) and came within three games of winning the '67 pennant. What was Stanky's nickname?

CHICAGO WHITE SOX

A12   The Hitless Wonders

A13   Les O'Connor (The AL commissioner fined the GM $500 for improperly signing a Chicago prep pitcher. When O'Connor refused to pay, the league officer evicted the club. The team was reinstated a day later when Chuck Comiskey paid the fine.)

A14   The Cleveland Indians
The St. Louis Browns

A15   In 1947, Larry Doby was the first black player to ink a contract in the AL. Veeck signed 48-year-old rookie Satchel Paige to a deal in 1948.

A16   The 3-foot-7 Gaedel batted as a pinch hitter for Veeck's St. Louis Browns.

A17   1958   (He bought 58 percent of the club's stock from Dorothy Comiskey.)

A18   The Artnell Corporation

A19   One of his used wooden legs

A20   John Allyn

A21   Edward DeBartolo

A22   Baltimore (1955–61)

A23   The Cleveland Indians

A24   Casey Stengel (The Yankees won the AL pennant from 1949 through 1953 and from 1955 through 1958.)

A25   The Brat

*** SOX FAST FACTS ***

Outfielder Frank Huelsman (1904) has the dubious distinction of being the first AL player to play for four clubs in one season: Chicago (four games), Detroit (four games), St. Louis (20 games), and Washington (84 games). His total major league career consisted of three seasons and five teams.

Q26 Name the three men who held the Sox manager's post during the 1968 season.

Q27 Prior to managing Chicago, Jeff Torborg was at Cleveland's helm from June 19, 1977, until July 23, 1979. Who did he replace as the Indians' manager?

Q28 Don Zimmer was one of three baseball managers to get the ax within a three-day period in 1991. Name the other two deposed skippers.

Q29 Jim Essian played in the big leagues with the Sox, Philadelphia, Seattle, Cleveland, and Oakland over his 12-year career. What position did he play most of the time?

Q30 Jeff Torborg caught two no-hitters while playing for the Dodgers. Name the pitchers who were involved in those games.

Q31 While playing for California, Torborg caught a no-hitter. Who was his battery mate?

Q32 The Sox's traveling secretary was voted the best batting practice pitcher in the majors by *Sports Illustrated* in 1983. Name him.

Q33 Before being named manager of the Sox in 1991, Gene Lamont was a member of the Pirate coaching staff. What position did he coach with Pittsburgh for five years?

Q34 Gene Lamont's big league career lasted a mere 87 games. For what team did he play?

Q35 In his first major league at-bat, Gene Lamont swatted a home run against Boston. Who was on the mound for the Red Sox?

THE UNIFORMS

Q1 Name the three Hall of Famers who spent their entire professional career with the White Sox.

Q2 What former Pale Hoser was the first Chicago player elected to the Baseball Hall of Fame?

Q3 Name the two Sox players who have been selected American League Most Valuable Players.

CHICAGO WHITE SOX

A26   Eddie Stanky
        Les Moss
        Al Lopez

A27   Frank Robinson

A28   Kansas City's John Wathan
        Baltimore's Frank Robinson

A29   Catcher

A30   Sandy Koufax (1965)
        Bill Singer (1970)

A31   Nolan Ryan (1973)

A32   Glen Rosenbaum

A33   Third base

A34   The Detroit Tigers

A35   Cal Koonce

A1   Ted Lyons (1923–42, 1946)
       Red Faber (1914–33)
       Luke Appling (1930–50)

A2   Eddie Collins (1939)

A3   Nellie Fox (1959)
       Dick Allen (1972)

*** SOX FAST FACTS ***

Wilson Alvarez was the first player born in the 1970s to throw a no-hitter in the majors.

Q4 The last AL second baseman to be named Most Valuable Player was a member of the White Sox. Who was so honored in 1959?

Q5 Between 1956 and 1985, the Sox accounted for five of the American League's Rookies of the Year. Name the recipients of the annual honor.

Q6 Name the Pale Hoser who started in five straight All-Star Games—the most consecutive appearances of any Sox player.

Q7 The first All-Star team was selected in 1933. Name the two players who represented the Sox that year.

Q8 Who was the last White Sox pitcher to lead the American League in winning percentage?

Q9 Who was the last Sox pitcher to lead the American League in ERA?

Q10 Who was the last Sox hurler to lead the league in strikeouts?

Q11 Who led Chicago and the league in winning percentage during the team's first season of 1901?

Q12 Who was the winning pitcher in the inaugural game for the Sox, and the American League, on April 24, 1901?

Q13 What early-day Sox pitcher is generally regarded as having invented the spitball?

Q14 What pitcher was known for his "flutterball"?

Q15 The 1901 league leader in walks (86), he was known for his swift baserunning. He played only a single season with the White Stockings, but gained notoriety some 80 years later when a stage play was written about him. Who was this outfielder?

Q16 In the club's first year, this White Sox player led the league in stolen bases with 48. Who was he?

Q17 The first Sox pitcher to toss a no-hitter also threw the team's initial one-hitter, the season before. Name this utility player.

Q18 The first major league game that Hall of Fame pitcher Ed Walsh played was in relief on May 12, 1904, in Philadelphia. Who did he replace on the mound that game?

Q19 What member of the Hitless Wonders led AL pitchers in both earned run average and games lost in 1910?

CHICAGO WHITE SOX

A4   Nellie Fox

A5   1956: Luis Aparicio
1963: Gary Peters
1966: Tommie Agee
1983: Ron Kittle
1985: Ozzie Guillen

A6   Nellie Fox (1955–59. He also started in 1951 and 1963.)

A7   Al Simmons (starter)
Jimmy Dykes

A8   Richard Dotson (1983:22–7, .759)

A9   Joel Horlen (1967: 2.06)

A10   Early Wynn (1958: 179)

A11   Clark Griffith (24–7, .774)

A12   Roy Patterson

A13   Ed Walsh

A14   Hoyt Wilhelm

A15   William Ellsworth "Dummy" Hoy (Hoy was a deaf mute. The play for which he was an inspiration was titled *The Single Season of Dummy Hoy.*)

A16   Frank Isbell

A17   Jim "Nixey" Callahan (September 20, 1902: 3–0 vs. Detroit)

A18   Guy "Doc" White

A19   Ed Walsh

*** SOX FAST FACTS ***

Since 1900, Jimmie Dykes (1935–46) is one of two men to manage six different clubs in his career. The other is Dick Williams.

Q20 Incredibly, Joe Jackson batted .408 in his first complete season in the majors, but he did not win the batting crown. Who copped the honors with a .420 average?

Q21 Who did Joe Jackson replace in left field when he came to Chicago in 1915?

Q22 How did Joe Jackson obtain the moniker "Shoeless"?

Q23 The night before the first game of the 1919 World Series, Shoeless Joe met with Charles Comiskey. Why did Jackson meet with the club owner?

Q24 The character of Shoeless Joe Jackson was featured in two movies, *Eight Men Out* and *Field of Dreams*. Who portrayed Jackson in the films?

Q25 On September 11, 1912, this player stole six bases in a single game. Eleven days later, he did it again. Who was this fearless thief?

Q26 This future Hall of Famer made his major league debut with the Sox on August 20, 1913. Unfortunately, he failed to impress the Pale Hose front office. After returning to the minors, he was claimed by the Giants. Name this all-time great.

Q27 How many times did Eddie Collins lead the AL in fielding?

Q28 Of his 25 seasons in the majors, how many years with a .300-plus batting average did Eddie Collins enjoy?

Q29 What was Hall of Famer Eddie Collins's nickname?

Q30 Name the pitcher whose perfect game, a 2–0 victory, led the Sox over the Detroit Tigers on April 30, 1922.

Q31 Name the Hall of Fame pitcher who came straight from Baylor University to the White Sox clubhouse in 1923.

Q32 What early-day player put to rest any unflattering theories about the intelligence of catchers when he earned degrees from Princeton and the Sorbonne and proved he was fluent in seven languages?

Q33 In 1923, this team made Ted Lyons an offer he could refuse. Instead, the Hall of Famer signed with Chicago for $300 a month and a $1,000 bonus. What club was unable to lure Lyons to their line up?

Q34 A White Sox infielder was the first player to homer in his first major league at-bat. Who clubbed the famous dinger on July 17, 1930?

CHICAGO WHITE SOX

A20   Ty Cobb

A21   Chano Collins

A22   Because of a blister on his foot, Jackson went to bat in an exhibition game in his stocking feet. He hit a homer, and as he circled the bases, a fan shouted, "You, Shoeless Joe." The name stuck.

A23   He wanted to be taken out of the lineup.

A24   *Eight Men Out:* D. B. Sweeney
         Field of Dreams: Ray Liotta

A25   Eddie Collins

A26   Edd Roush (The Giants traded him to the Cincinnati Reds, and he went on to play 17 major league seasons with a .323 average.)

A27   Nine

A28   19

A29   "Cocky"

A30   Charlie Robertson

A31   Ted Lyons

A32   Moe Berg (1926–30)

A33   The Philadelphia A's

A34   Blondy Ryan

*** SOX FAST FACTS ***

"HE REFUSED TO BECOME INVOLVED UNTIL..."
First baseman Zeke Bonura (1934–37) led the American League in fielding for his position in 1936 because he would let easy grounders go by him without a play. Though colorful and a slugger (27 dingers in his rookie season), he was eventually traded because of his interest in making a play for owner J. Lou Comiskey's daughter.

THE UNIFORMS

Q35 Name the player who backed up Sox Hall of Fame catcher Ray Schalk for eight seasons.

Q36 What was Luke Appling's nickname?

Q37 Who ended Appling's club-record 27-game hitting streak on September 3, 1936?

Q38 Luke Appling had an amazing run up the middle for the Sox, lasting 20 years as the team's shortstop. Who replaced the Hall of Famer in 1950?

Q39 During a 1982 old-timers' game, Luke Appling, at age 75, blasted a home run in Washington's JFK Stadium. Name the Hall of Famer who tossed the memorable pitch.

Q40 A five-year veteran of the club, this pitcher shot himself in a hunting accident. His leg was amputated, and after he was fitted with an artificial leg, he played in the minors for a year and won 18 games. Who was he?

Q41 Why was Ted Lyons called a "Sunday pitcher"?

Q42 Ted Lyons's 260th victory was recorded on April 28, 1946, with a 4–3 decision. Against what club did the Hall of Famer register his last win?

Q43 Who belted six singles in six at-bats in a game on July 22, 1962?

Q44 How many consecutive seasons did Nellie Fox lead the AL in fewest strikeouts?

Q45 Second baseman Nellie Fox had a .998 fielding percentage in 1963. Who is the only Sox player at that position to match his fielding percentage since then?

Q46 What club rejected Nellie Fox after he had three unproductive seasons and then sent him packing to Chicago?

Q47 In his first game with the Sox, on May 1, 1951, Minnie Minoso hit a home run in his first at-bat. Who was on the hill for the Yankees?

Q48 In the same game that Minnie Minoso collected his first Chicago homer, a future Hall of Famer belted his first major league four-bagger. Name the slugger.

Q49 How old was Minnie Minoso when Bill Veeck brought the outfielder back for three games in 1980?

Q50 What Hall of Fame player was lost by the White Sox in the 1969 expansion draft?

CHICAGO WHITE SOX

A35   Bucky Crouse

A36   "Old Aches and Pains"

A37   Boston's Wes Farrell

A38   Chico Carrasquel (1950–56)

A39   Warren Spahn

A40   Monty Stratton

A41   Near the end of the 1930s, Lyons always pitched on Sunday, because the largest crowds turned out on that day.

A42   The St. Louis Cardinals

A43   Floyd Robinson (vs. Boston)

A44   11 (1952–62)

A45   Scott Fletcher (1990)

A46   The Philadelphia A's (1947–49)

A47   Vic Raschi

A48   Mickey Mantle

A49   60

A50   Hoyt Wilhelm (to the Kansas City Royals)

*** SOX FAST FACTS ***

WHITE SOX TEAM SEASON BATTING RECORDS
Most Runs—920 (1936)
Most HRs—192 (1977)
Most Grand Slams—7 (1961)
Most RBIs—862 (1936)
Most Strikeouts—1,023 (1985)
Highest Batting Average—.295 (1920)
Most Consecutive Games/Home Runs—16 (32 HRs; 1983)

Q8 (The Suits). Charles Comiskey was a player-manager for the St. Louis Browns of the American Association in the late 1800s. What innovation did the first baseman bring to the game?

CHICAGO WHITE SOX

Q26 (Setting the Standard). On May 11, 1990, Bobby Thigpen became the Sox's all-time save leader while earning his ninety-ninth save against Kansas City. Whose record did he break?

Q43 (FYI). The final game at old Comiskey Park was held on September 30, 1990. What Sox pitcher won that final game?

THE UNIFORMS

Q51 On the last day of the 1971 season, Bill Melton hit his 33rd dinger to capture the American League home run title. Who gave up the round-tripper?

Q52 In 1972 and 1973, this Chicago player led the American League in both wins and innings pitched. Who is he?

Q53 Name the pitching pair that combined to toss a no-hitter against the Oakland A's on July 28, 1976.

Q54 What White Sox speedster was given exclusive rights among athletes to use the copyrighted nickname "Road Runner" by Warner Brothers?

Q55 Name the promising young pitcher whose life was cut short in a 1969 automobile accident.

Q56 In 1980, two Sox rookies posted 10-plus wins during the season. Name the combo.

Q57 Despite a strike-shortened season in 1981 (88 games), Tim Raines set a rookie record with 71 steals. Name the two first-year pros who have since broken Raines's mark.

Q58 Identify the player wielding this hot bat: In a 1982 game against Detroit, he hit three consecutive home runs, including a grand slam, to lead the Sox over the Tigers, 7–0.

Q59 Tom Seaver's 300th victory took place on August 4, 1985. What club did he defeat to reach that plateau?

Q60 What was the only major league team that Seaver never defeated during his stellar career?

Q61 On August 17, 1986, Seaver recorded victory number 311, his final win. What team did he conquer?

Q62 Tom Seaver ended his career with a 311–205 record and an ERA of 2.86. What three modern-day major league pitchers have had a better ERA (minimum: 3,000 innings)?

Q63 On the same day that Seaver registered his 300th victory, another major leaguer ripped his 3,000th hit. Who is he?

Q64 What two pitchers have more career strikeouts than Tom Terrific?

Q65 How many times has Tom Seaver won the Cy Young Award?

CHICAGO WHITE SOX

A51 Milwaukee's Bill Parsons

A52 Wilbur Wood (1972: 24–17; 377 innings)
             (1973: 24–20; 359 innings)

A53 John Odom
           Francisco Barrios
           (Chicago edged the A's, 2–1.)

A54 Ralph Garr

A55 Paul Edmonson

A56 Britt Burns (15–13)
           Richard Dotson (12–10)

A57 Juan Samuel (1984: 72)
           Vince Coleman (1985: 110)

A58 Harold Baines

A59 The Yankees, in New York (on "Phil Rizzuto Day" at Yankee Stadium)

A60 The Toronto Blue Jays

A61 The Minnesota Twins (at the Metrodome)

A62 Walter Johnson (2.37)
           Grover Cleveland Alexander (2.56)
           Whitey Ford (2.74)

A63 Rod Carew

A64 Nolan Ryan
           Steve Carlton

A65 Three (1969, 1973, 1975)

*** SOX FAST FACTS ***

WHITE SOX OPENING DAYS
Widest Opening Day Shutout Margins:
Detroit 16, SOX 0; 4/18/91
Sox 14, Texas 0; 4/18/72

Q66 Tim Raines has garnered both the National League batting crown (1986: .334) and stolen base title (1981: 71; 1982: 78; 1983: 90, 1984: 75) in his career. Who was the last player to do this before Raines?

Q67 On July 22, 1987, Harold Baines hit his 155th Chicago dinger to become the club's all-time home run hitter (He has since been surpassed.) What pitcher gave up the homer, and who held the club title prior to Baines?

Q68 Following his trade to Texas, the White Sox retired Harold Baines's uniform number. Only two other players have had their numbers retired while they were still active in the major leagues. Who are they?

Q69 Who led the 1988 Sox in hitting with a .303 average—the only Pale Hoser to stroke .300 that season?

Q70 What Sox player starred in a Venezuelan soap opera in 1989?

Q71 This 1990 Sox acquisition left the United States to play for the Yokohama Whales in Japan and became the first player to be featured in Tokyo's first-ever card and memorabilia show. Who is he?

Q72 Who tossed a rain-shortened no-hitter (six innings) against the Yankees in New York on July 12, 1990?

Q73 This Sox player fouled off 24 percent of the pitches thrown to him in the 1990 season, the highest rate in the majors. Name him.

Q74 Though a no-hitter was tossed against them on July 1, 1990, the Sox defeated the Yankees 4–0. Who was the winning pitcher in this strange affair?

Q75 Who was the only Sox player to have more walks (55) than strikeouts (53) in the 1990 season?

Q76 How many errors did Ozzie Guillen commit when he won his first Gold Glove Award in 1990?

Q77 Who was the only American Leaguer to reach double figures in doubles (26), triples (10), and home runs (15) in 1990?

Q78 This Auburn alumnus entered college on a football scholarship and played receiver on the same team as Bo Jackson before turning to baseball full-time. Name the player who set school records for career homers (49) and single-season walks (73).

Q79 Name the Pale Hoser who earned national attention when he registered a 58-game hitting streak as a sophomore at Oklahoma State.

CHICAGO WHITE SOX

A66   Willie Mays

A67   Baltimore's Mike Boddicker gave up the hit that allowed Baines to pass Bill Melton.

A68   Frank Robinson (retired by Baltimore in 1972 while he was playing for the Dodgers)
Phil Niekro (retired in 1984 while he was playing for the Yankees)

A69   Dave Gallagher

A70   Ozzie Guillen

A71   Phil Bradley

A72   Melido Perez

A73   Ozzie Guillen

A74   Barry Jones (Greg Hibbard started and pitched a no-hitter until the sixth, and Jones came in to relieve.)

A75   Robin Ventura

A76   17

A77   Sammy Sosa

A78   Frank Thomas

A79   Robin Ventura

*** SOX FAST FACTS ***

THE WORLD OF "LITTLE LOOIE"—LUIS APARICIO
Holds lifetime shortstop records for games, double plays, and assists as well as American League records for putouts and total chances. Named Rookie of the Year in 1956, he led the AL in stolen bases nine straight years and led AL shortstops eight years in fielding, seven times in assists, four times in putouts, and twice each in total chances per game and double plays.

Q80 What is the name of the album Jack McDowell released with his band, V.I.E.W.?

Q81 This pitcher graduated from Evergreen High and had an outstanding career at the University of Illinois. Who is this local product?

Q82 He became the first pitcher since Dwight Gooden to gain a spot on a major league roster after playing the previous season in Class A ball. Name him.

Q83 Ron Kittle was signed to his third Sox contract on June 19, 1991. What five clubs has he played with since 1987?

Q84 How many separate tenures did Ron Kittle have with the White Sox?

Q85 It wasn't the moon over Miami when Steve Lyons dropped his drawers in a July 1990 game. Who were the Chisox playing when Psycho lost his head and his pants?

Q86 Who was the first Sox player to win a batting title?

Q87 Only one Sox player has led the American League in batting average. Who is he?

Q88 Name the four White Sox players who have hit inside-the-park grand slams.

Q89 On two occasions, players who have won the AL home run title have started the season with Chicago and then been traded in midterm. Name the players.

Q90 Who are the only pair of Sox to lead the American League in home runs for a season?

Q91 Who is the oldest player to hit 20 or more home runs in a season for the White Sox?

Q92 Name the 1901 player who led the Sox with five homers in the club's first year of existence.

Q93 Two Chicago players, Herm McFarland and Billy Sullivan, led the 1901 White Sox in home runs. How many did each player poke?

Q94 Who hit the Sox's first inside-the-park homer?

Q95 In Carlton Fisk's first game with the White Sox, he belted a three-run homer to lead Chicago to a 5–3 victory. Who were the Sox playing?

CHICAGO WHITE SOX

A80 *Extendagenda*

A81 Donn Pall

A82 Scott Radinsky

A83 Yankees (1987)
Indians (1988)
Sox (1989, 1991)
Orioles (1990)
Indians (1991—released in April)

A84 Three (1983–86; 1989; 1990)

A85 Detroit

A86 Luke Appling (1936: .388)

A87 Luke Appling (1936: .388; 1943: .328)

A88 Ferris Fain (June 16, 1954: vs. Philadelphia at Comiskey)
Carlos May (September 18, 1971: vs. California at Comiskey)
Ron Santo (June 9, 1974: vs. Boston at Comiskey)
Ron Karkovice (August 29, 1990: vs. Minnesota at Metrodome)

A89 Robert "Braggo" Roth (1915: Chicago and Cleveland)
Gus Zernial (1951: Chicago and Philadelphia)

A90 Bill Melton (1971: 33)
Dick Allen (1972: 37; 1974: 32)

A91 Carlton Fisk (In 1987, at age 39, he hit 23 dingers.)

A92 Sam Mertes

A93 Four

A94 Ed Mulligan (June 3, 1921: vs. Washington at Griffith Stadium)

A95 The Boston Red Sox (April 10, 1981: at Fenway)

Q96   In his first home game at Comiskey, Fisk hit a grand slam and led the Sox to a 9–3 win over Milwaukee. Name the pitcher who gave up the four-run dinger.

Q97   Of Fisk's 37 home runs in 1985, 33 of them came while he was catching, thus breaking an American League single-season record for homers by a catcher. Whose mark of 32 round-trippers did he break?

Q98   Who gave up Fisk's 300th dinger on September 5, 1987?

Q99   Carlton Fisk set a major league standard for catchers when he swatted his 328th homer on August 17, 1990. What player did he surpass?

Q100   What pitcher gave up Carlton Fisk's record-breaking 328th home run?

Q101   Carlton Fisk is just the third catcher in modern baseball history to swat 300 homers, score 1,000 runs, and accumulate 1,000 RBIs. Who are the other two?

Q102   The same blast that established Carlton Fisk as the all-time home run leader among major league catchers also made the 43-year-old the all-time White Sox home run hitter. Whose club mark did Fisk smash?

Q103   At 43, Carlton Fisk was the oldest player to suit up in the 1991 All-Star Game. Name the two players who were older than Fisk when they played in the midsummer classic.

Q104   Name the Hall of Fame pitcher who has given up seven home runs—the most of any pitcher—to Carlton Fisk.

Q105   What record did Bo Jackson tie in the 1989 All-Star Game?

Q106   Who is Steve Joyce?

Q107   Bo's return to major league baseball took place on September 2, 1991, against his old team, the Royals. Who did Jackson ground out to in his first at-bat?

Q108   What is Bo Jackson's given name?

Q109   Bo Jackson's uniform number in both football and baseball was 34. When Jackson joined the Chisox, he was given No. 8. Who said he would not relinquish No. 34 for Bo?

CHICAGO WHITE SOX

A96   Pete Vuckovich (April 14, 1981)

A97   Lance Parrish's (for Detroit in 1982)

A98   Kansas City's Danny Jackson

A99   Cincinnati's Johnny Bench

A100   Texas's Charlie Hough

A101   Yogi Berra
Johnny Bench

A102   Harold Baines's (186 homers)

A103   Satchel Paige, who was 47, was named to play in the 1953 game.
Pete Rose was selected to play in the 1985 game at the age of 44.

A104   Jim Palmer

A105   He hit a home run in his first at-bat.

A106   The Royals' doctor who said that Bo Jackson's baseball career was over.

A107   Pitcher Luis Aquino (For the game, Jackson went 0 for 3 with a sacrifice fly.)

A108   Vincent

A109   Ken Patterson

_____   .   _____

*** SOX FAST FACTS ***

Besides being an infielder and manager with the White Sox, Russ
Blackburne's greatest contribution to baseball may be his discovery
and marketing of mud from the Delaware River, which was used by
umpires to rub the gloss off new balls.

SETTING THE STANDARD

Q1 What is the club record for consecutive victories?

Q2 What is the team record for consecutive losses?

Q3 In what year did the Sox start off the season with eight straight wins—the most in team history?

Q4 The lowly 1968 Sox established two team records of dubious distinction—consecutive losses at the start of the season and consecutive scoreless innings. What are these records?

Q5 On April 23, 1955, the Sox were unstoppable as they ran up a score of 29–6 and established a number of offensive records. Who did they demolish?

Q6 The 1917 Sox established a team record when they won 100 games (against 54 losses). What team did they defeat on September 29, 1917, to register their 100th win?

Q7 This White Sox pitcher struck out seven consecutive batters to establish an American League record. Who was he?

Q8 This South Side pitcher was the oldest player to lead the AL in both starts (40) and innings (285.1) for a season. Name him.

Q9 This Sox hurler set a club mark for both consecutive scoreless innings (45) and lowest earned run average (1.52). Who was he?

Q10 Name the Chisox player who set a major league record for shutouts by a rookie.

Q11 Name the only Sox pitchers who have had four seasons with 20 or more wins.

Q12 Who threw the only perfect game for the White Sox?

Q13 Who holds the major league record for most no-hitters caught?

Q14 What pitcher has been with the White Sox for the most seasons, holds the club record for most wins and most losses, and has pitched the most innings?

Q15 Name the Chicago pitcher who set a team record for futility by losing 14 consecutive games.

Q16 The Sox record for most strikeouts in a single game is 16. What hurler established the mark?

CHICAGO WHITE SOX

A1   19 (August 2–23, 1906)

A2   13 (August 9–26, 1924)

A3   1982 (April 11–18)

A4   Losses to start the season: 10
Consecutive scoreless innings: 39 (May 22–26, 1968. Later in the same season, from July 21 to 25, the Sox went 37 innings without a run.)

A5   The Kansas City A's (at K.C.)

A6   The New York Yankees

A7   Joe Cowley (May 28, 1986: at Texas)

A8   Charlie Hough (1987—at age 39 years, 9 months)

A9   Guy "Doc" White

A10   Ewell Russell (1913: eight)

A11   Ed Walsh
Urban "Red" Faber
Wilbur Wood

A12   Charles Robertson (April 30, 1922: vs. Detroit)

A13   Ray "Cracker" Schalk, with four (two in 1914; one in 1917; one in 1922)

A14   Ted Lyons (1923–42, 1946: 21 seasons; 260 wins and 230 losses; 4,161 innings)

A15   Howie Judson (1949)

A16   Jack Harshman (July 25, 1954: at Boston)

*** SOX FAST FACTS ***

Moe Berg—"He can speak 12 languages but can't hit in any of them."
Sox infielder Moe Berg was an alumnus of three universities, a lawyer, mathematician, and linguist, and was used as a spy by the U.S. government prior to World War II. Despite his intelligence and daring, he batted only .243 over a 15-year major league career.

SETTING THE STANDARD

Q17 Name the pitcher who set a club record by starting in seven season openers for the White Sox.

Q18 Name the Sox player who etched his name in the record books when he was beaned 23 times in a season.

Q19 Who was the first reliever to win an ERA title in the majors?

Q20 Who holds the team record with 15 relief wins in one year?

Q21 Three Sox pitchers opened their season with nine consecutive wins. Name the players who are tied for this club record.

Q22 Name the minor leaguer who made history in 1989 by tossing three no-hitters, including two consecutively.

Q23 In 1990, Sox relievers broke a major league save record with 68. What team had held the record with 64 saves?

Q24 During the 1988 season, Bobby Thigpen set a new Sox mark (which he later broke; see Q25) by garnering 34 saves. Name the previous holder of this club record.

Q25 Thigpen racked up a remarkable 57 saves in the 1990 season. How many opportunities did Thiggy have in his record-setting campaign?

Q26 On May 11, 1990, Bobby Thigpen became the Sox's all-time save leader while earning his 99th save against Kansas City. Whose record did he break?

Q27 Thigpen established a new major league single-season record by recording 57 saves during 1990. Whose old record of 46 did he surpass?

Q28 What streak started on May 15, 1941, when the Sox demolished the Yankees, 13–1?

Q29 Name the Sox player who holds a club record for most hits in a season—222.

Q30 Name the Sox player who established an American League record for shortstops with a season batting average of .388.

Q31 In the question cited above, was that the first batting crown captured by a White Sox player?

Q32 Name the three Sox who have swatted six hits in a single game.

CHICAGO WHITE SOX

A17   Billy Pierce

A18   Minnie Minoso (1956)

A19   Hoyt Wilhelm (1952: in his rookie year while pitching for the New York Giants)

A20   Eddie Fisher (1965)

A21   Lefty Williams (1917)
Orval Grove (1943)
LaMarr Hoyt (1982)

A22   Vancouver's Tom Drees (He equaled a pro mark set by "A" ball pitcher Bill Bell in 1952.)

A23   The 1988 Oakland A's

A24   Bob James (1985: 32 saves)

A25   65

A26   Hoyt Wilhelm's (98)

A27   Dave Righetti of the Yankees (1986)

A28   That contest was the beginning of Joe DiMaggio's 56-game hitting streak.

A29   Eddie Collins (1920)

A30   Luke Appling (1936)

A31   Yes

A32   Hank Steinbacher (June 22, 1938: vs. Washington)
Rip Radcliff (July 18, 1936: vs. Philadelphia)
Floyd Robinson (July 22, 1962: vs. Boston)

SETTING THE STANDARD

Q33 On September 2, 1937, the White Sox became the first team to lead off a game with two home runs. Name the Chicago players who belted the dingers at Comiskey.

Q34 Who is the only Sox player to belt four homers in a game?

Q35 Name the Chicago player who belted three grand slams in one year, setting a White Sox record.

Q36 Who set the club record for most homers in a month—13—in July 1972?

Q37 The club record for home runs in a season is 37 and was set by two right-handed batters, Dick Allen (1972) and Carlton Fisk (1985). Who holds the Sox HR record for lefties?

Q38 Name the three Sox players who combined for 93 home runs during the 1983 season—the most ever by a Pale Hose trio in one year.

Q39 Who established the club's rookie home run record by swatting 35 dingers in his first major league season?

Q40 Name the Sox slugger who holds the American League record for consecutive games (13) with an RBI.

Q41 True or false. Carlton Fisk was the first player ever to snare the Rookie of the Year award unanimously.

Q42 The 1991 All-Star Game at the Toronto Skydome was the setting as Carlton Fisk became the oldest player to stroke a hit in the midsummer classic. He was 43 years, six months old, when he singled in the sixth inning. Who held the record before Fisk?

Q43 Who set a Sox record when he stole 77 bases in a season?

Q44 What Chicago player broke Rollie Zeider's AL rookie record for steals— 46—in 1986?

Q45 Only once since 1902 have the Sox had three players who have stolen 30 or more bases in a season. Name the 1990 players who did it.

Q46 In 1990, at age 30, Tim Raines became the second-youngest major leaguer to record 600 stolen bases. Who reached that plateau at a younger age?

CHICAGO WHITE SOX

A33 Boze Berger and Mike Kreevich (vs. Boston)

A34 Pat Seerey (July 18, 1948: at Philadelphia)

A35 Pete Ward (1964)

A36 Dick Allen

A37 Oscar Gamble (1977: 31 HRs)

A38 Ron Kittle (35)
Greg Luzinski (32)
Carlton Fisk (26)

A39 Ron Kittle (1983)

A40 Taft Wright (May 4–20, 1941)

A41 True (1972)

A42 Ted Williams (who was 41 years, 10 months old, when he hit safely in the 1960 All-Star Game)

A43 Rudy Law (1983)

A44 John Cangelosi

A45 Lance Johnson (36)
Ivan Calderon (32)
Sammy Sosa (32)

A46 Rickey Henderson (at age 28)

*** SOX FAST FACTS ***

Ron Blomberg (1978) was baseball's first designated hitter on Opening Day, 1973, while with the Yankees.

SETTING THE STANDARD

Q47   The Sox record for single-season strikeouts by a batter is 175. Who holds this dubious mark?

Q48   Name the only two Pale Hosers who have appeared in every game during a single season.

Q49   Who set Chicago's single-season shortstop record for assists with 570 in one year?

Q50   The longest game in American League history started on May 10, 1984, and ended the following day at Comiskey Park. Who did the Sox defeat, 5–4, in 25 innings?

Q51   In the marathon game cited in the previous question, who was the Chicago pitcher of record?

Q52   In 1984's classic 25-inning game, who ripped a homer to end it?

FYI

Q1   At what location in Chicago was the American League created in the winter of 1899–1900?

Q2   How many times have the White Sox landed in the AL cellar?

Q3   Cub owner James Hart permitted the White Stockings to play in Chicago at the turn of the century in return for two considerations. What were they?

Q4   The Sox were on the losing end of the only Opening Day no-hitter in major league history as this Cleveland pitcher put his name in the record books on April 16, 1940. Who was the Indian hurler?

Q5   The color barrier was broken in the American League on July 5, 1947, at Comiskey Park. Name the Cleveland Indian who made history when he stepped up to the plate as a pinch hitter.

Q6   The largest crowd the Sox ever played before was 78,382. Where were the South Siders playing?

Q7   In a 1959 game, the Sox routed the Kansas City A's by a 20–6 score merely on Johnny Callison's single in the seventh inning. How did Callison's single result in 11 runs?

CHICAGO WHITE SOX

A47 Dave Nicholson (1963)

A48 Don Buford (1966)
Greg Walker (1985)

A49 Ozzie Guillen (1988. He surpassed Luis Aparicio's mark of 563, set in
1969.)

A50 The Milwaukee Brewers

A51 Tom Seaver

A52 Harold Baines

A1 The Grand Northern Hotel

A2 Six (1924, 1931, 1934, 1948, 1968, 1989)

A3 The Stockings' owner had to agree to locate the team south of 35th
Street, and he could not use the city's name in identifying the club.

A4 Bob Feller (The score was 1–0.)

A5 Larry Doby

A6 Cleveland Stadium (August 20, 1948)

A7 In the seventh, the Sox got 10 walks—five with the bases loaded—and
capitalized on three A's errors and a hit batsman.

*** SOX FAST FACTS ***

MOST RUNS IN AN OPENER:
Detroit 16, Sox 0; 4/18/91
Sox 17, St. Louis 3; 4/17/51

Q8   Chicago has registered 15 doubleheader shutouts in franchise history. The last one took place on September 10, 1967. Who did the Sox meet that afternoon?

Q9   During the 1968 and '69 seasons, the Sox played some of their home games out of town. Where was the alternate home field?

Q10   The White Sox remain the last major league club to open a season with a scheduled doubleheader. Whom did they defeat in their April 7, 1971, twin bill, 6–5 and 12–4?

Q11   What was the nickname of the 1977 Sox?

Q12   After playing in a 1978 game against the White Sox, this Angel was shot and killed while visiting his hometown of Gary, Indiana. Who was he?

Q13   The White Sox established a major league record when they won the division in 1983 by a 20-game margin. Who was the runner-up to Chicago in the AL's Western Division that season?

Q14   In 1933, Comiskey Park was the site of the first All-Star Game. What other world-famous event was in progress at the same time?

Q15   Name the Yankee pitcher who threw a no-hitter against the Sox on July 1, 1990, in a losing effort.

Q16   Who hit Chicago's first grand slam at the new Comiskey Park? (Hint: It was his first career slam.)

Q17   Who pitched the only perfect game against the Sox?

Q18   Who holds the record for single-season home runs at old Comiskey?

Q19   What had to be installed in the original Comiskey Park to accommodate 300-pound owner Lou Comiskey?

Q20   The facility in which the Sox first played was a wooden stadium located at 39th and Wentworth streets. What sport was played there before Charles Comiskey renovated it?

Q21   Where did the Sox call home prior to the opening of Comiskey in 1910?

Q22   Comiskey Park opened on July 1, 1910, to a full house, but the Sox made an inauspicious start with a 2–0 loss. Who whitewashed the club that day?

CHICAGO WHITE SOX

A8 The Detroit Tigers (Chicago won 6–0 and 4–0.)

A9 County Stadium (Milwaukee)

A10 The Oakland A's (The A's opened the season two days before at Washington.)

A11 The South Side Hitmen (They hit a club-record 192 homers that season.)

A12 Lyman Bostock

A13 Kansas City

A14 The Chicago World's Fair

A15 Andy Hawkins (Chicago won 4–0 thanks to three eighth-inning errors by the Yankees.)

A16 Robin Ventura (The Sox edged the Indians, 6–5, on June 18, 1991.)

A17 Cleveland's Adrian Joss (October 2, 1908)

A18 Dick Allen (1972: 27)

A19 An elevator

A20 Cricket (It was home to the Chicago Wanderers Cricket Club.)

A21 South Side Park

A22 The St. Louis Browns

*** SOX FAST FACTS ***

CARLTON FISK—FROM NO. 27 TO NO. 72
When he signed with Chicago, Carlton Fisk altered his uniform number from 27 to 72. He gave three reasons for the change:
—1972 was the year his son Casey was born
—it was his rookie year in the majors
—the change of clubs represented a turnaround in his career

Q23 The first Chicago home run in old Comiskey was a grand slam against the Detroit Tigers on July 31, 1910. Who hit the four-run blast?

Q24 What is the Legend of the Lucky Brick?

Q25 The first batter to hit a Comiskey "roof shot" home run did it on August 16, 1927, against the White Sox. Who was he?

Q26 The number of old Comiskey roof shots increased dramatically in 1983: While only 21 were hit in the first 72 years, 23 homers cleared the roof in the following eight seasons. What accounted for the rise?

Q27 What pitcher gave up the most roof shots at old Comiskey?

Q28 Who was the winning pitcher in the 1933 All-Star Game held at Comiskey Park?

Q29 The first major league All-Star Game was played at Comiskey Park on July 6, 1933. Whose two-run homer led the American League to a 4–2 victory over the National League?

Q30 Who was the first Pale Hoser to hit a roof shot at old Comiskey?

Q31 The Sox defeated the Cubs, 4–1, in an exhibition game at Wrigley Field. The game marked the first time a baseball game was televised (WGN). In what year did the broadcast take place?

Q32 The first Chicago night game was played at Comiskey Park on August 14, 1939. Who did the Sox defeat that evening by a score of 5–2?

Q33 It wasn't until 1949 that a Chicago player poked an inside-the-park homer at Comiskey. Name the Sox player who put his name in the record books.

Q34 How many World Series have been played at Comiskey Park?

Q35 In what year was the facade of old Comiskey Park painted white?

Q36 What was the AstroTurf in Comiskey Park nicknamed?

Q37 For seven seasons, the Sox "experimented" with AstroTurf before returning to the real thing. In what year was the synthetic grass installed in Comiskey?

Q38 What opposing team attracted the largest single-day attendance at Comiskey Park—55,555?

CHICAGO WHITE SOX

A23   Lee Tannehill

A24   During the construction of the ballpark in 1909–10, Charlie Comiskey painted a brick green and covered it with dirt. After the stadium was whitewashed in 1959, the brick could no longer be seen. Legend has it that Bill Veeck found the lucky brick, but it hasn't exactly been magical for the Sox. The club finished sixth the year it was buried.

A25   Babe Ruth (Chicago's Tommy Thomas gave up the dinger to the Bambino.)

A26   Home plate was moved eight feet closer to the outfield.

A27   Tom Seaver (He gave up four between 1984 and 1986.)

A28   Yankee Lefty Gomez

A29   Babe Ruth

A30   Eddie Robinson (April 25, 1951: off the St. Louis Browns' Al Widmar)

A31   1940 (April 16)

A32   The St. Louis Browns

A33   Luke Appling (May 13, 1949: vs. Cleveland)

A34   Four (1917, 1919, 1918 [Cubs vs. Boston], 1959)

A35   1960

A36   Sox Sod

A37   1969 (In 1976, natural grass again appeared in the park.)

A38   The Minnesota Twins (Sunday, May 20, 1973: doubleheader)

*** SOX FAST FACTS ***

Comiskey Chronology
Home To...First Exploding Scoreboard
The Majors' First All-Star Game
The Joe Louis Heavyweight Title Fight of 1937
The Beatles' Concert in 1965

Q39 On July 12, 1979, thousands of fans stormed the field at Comiskey Park during the infamous "Disco Demolition" promotion and caused the White Sox to forfeit the second game of a doubleheader after Chicago had dropped the first contest. Who was the team's opponent on that memorable evening?

Q40 In honor of the 50th Anniversary of the All-Star Game, the annual classic was held at the site of the original contest—Comiskey Park. Who belted a grand slam on July 6, 1983, to commemorate the game's golden anniversary?

Q41 The final Opening Day at old Comiskey Park took place on April 9, 1990. Who did the Sox defeat that day?

Q42 The final game at old Comiskey was held on September 30, 1990. Who did the Sox defeat, 2–1, that day?

Q43 What pitcher won that final game at old Comiskey?

Q44 Who was the last batter at old Comiskey?

Q45 Name the player who recorded the last putout in old Comiskey Park.

Q46 Who is Pete Johnson, and what role does he play in Comiskey Park history?

Q47 On the same day old Comiskey Park was torn down, another newsworthy event occurred in Sox history. What else happened on April 3, 1991?

Q48 The new Comiskey is the only major league park to face in a different direction from all other parks. In what direction does Comiskey face, and what is the "normal" direction?

Q49 The Sox's home opener at Comiskey II was memorable for the wrong reason: The Detroit Tigers creamed their hosts, 16–0. What Tiger pitcher made his first plate appearance after 19 years in the game?

Q50 What was the last baseball-only facility to be opened before Comiskey in 1991?

Q51 The White Sox's first game was an exhibition contest played on April 2, 1900, in Champaign, Illinois. Who did the club defeat by a score of 10–9?

Q52 The first regular-season game played by the Sox was a 5–4 loss. Who defeated the Windy City's newest franchise?

CHICAGO WHITE SOX

A39   The Detroit Tigers

A40   Fred Lynn (The American League prevailed, 13–3.)

A41   The Milwaukee Brewers (2–1)

A42   The Seattle Mariners

A43   Jack McDowell

A44   Seattle's Harold Reynolds

A45   Steve Lyons

A46   Johnson operated the wrecking ball that first struck Comiskey Park at 10:08 A.M. on April 3, 1991.

A47   The Sox signed Bo Jackson to a free agent contract.

A48   Comiskey faces southeast, while every other ballpark in major league baseball faces the traditional northeast.

A49   Frank Tanana (Donn Pall struck him out.)

A50   Kansas City's Royal Stadium (1972)

A51   The University of Illinois

A52   The Milwaukee Brewers (The Stockings' first win came against the same team the next day.)

*** SOX FAST FACTS ***

SINGLE-SEASON BATTING RECORDS
Average—Luke Appling (1936: .388)
RBIs—Zeke Bonura (1936: 138)
At-Bats—Nellie Fox (1956: 649)
Total Bases—Joe Jackson (1920: 336)
Runs—John Mostil (1925: 135)
Hits—Eddie Collins (1920: 222)
Strikeouts—Dave Nicholson (1963: 175)
Extra-Base Hits—Joe Jackson (1920: 74)
Home Runs—Carlton Fisk (1985: 37)
Pinch At-Bats—Smoky Burgess (1966: 66)

Q53 Who did the Stockings defeat to clinch the 1900 pennant?

Q54 The American League's first nine-inning no-hitter was thrown against the White Sox at Chicago on May 9, 1901. Who was credited with the no-no?

Q55 Name the *Chicago Tribune* editor who conceived of the idea of an All-Star Game.

Q56 What is the greatest number of losses ever suffered by a Sox club in a season?

Q57 What is the worst season that the Sox have had in terms of win-loss percentage?

GLORY DAYS

Q1 What Sox player is tied for a career World Series record with 14 stolen bases?

Q2 The Sox won the American League's first official pennant in 1901, but no World Series had yet developed between the rival leagues. Who did the Stockings meet in the "All American Series" that postseason?

Q3 The "Hitless Wonders" pulled off an upset of gigantic proportions when they defeated the Cubs for the 1906 crown. What little-used 31-year-old utilityman led the Sox in hitting?

Q4 Who poked the South Siders' only hit in Game 2 of the 1906 Series?

Q5 Who paced the South Siders to an 8–6 victory in Game 5 with a Series-record four doubles?

Q6 Name the Chicago pitcher who beat the Giants in Games 2, 5, and 6 of the 1917 World Series.

Q7 What famous athlete was listed as a starter in Game 5 of the 1917 World Series for the Giants, but was removed before he could make an appearance in the fall classic?

Q8 A Game 6 rundown was the most memorable play of the 1917 Series. Who crossed home plate for Chicago while the Giants inadvertently left it unattended?

CHICAGO WHITE SOX

A53   The Cleveland Blues (12–4)

A54   Cleveland's Earl Moore (Chicago won the game, 4–2, as both clubs were scoreless after nine innings. In the 10th inning, Chicago's Sandow Mertes singled, and the Sox went on to win with only two hits in the entire game.)

A55   Arch Ward

A56   106 (against 56 wins; 1970)

A57   1932 (49–102: .325)

A1   Eddie Collins (tied with Lou Brock)

A2   The AL All-Stars (led by Nap Lajoie)

A3   George Rohe (He replaced George Davis in the lineup and went 7 for 21, a .333 batting average.)

A4   Jiggs Donahue (in the seventh inning)

A5   Frank Isbell

A6   Red Faber (The Sox won the Series in six games.)

A7   Jim Thorpe (He was removed for a left-handed pinch hitter, Dave Robertson, in the top of the first inning. Thorpe was listed as the starting right fielder.)

A8   Eddie Collins

Q9   Interest in the 1919 World Series was so keen before its start that baseball officials changed its structure. How was it altered?

Q10   What baseball commissioner barred from organized ball for life the eight players implicated in the "Black Sox" scandal?

Q11   The first clue that the 1919 Series wasn't completely honest came before the start of the fall classic. What was the first hint?

Q12   Who were the eight "Black Sox" players?

Q13   Eddie Cicotte was Chicago's pitcher in the 1919 Series opener. What signal did he allegedly give to bettors that the fix was on?

Q14   Who hit the only home run of the 1919 World Series?

Q15   The Black Sox Series saw a pitcher lose three games in one World Series for the first time. Who established the record?

Q16   Cincinnati's batting leader (.357) in the 1919 Series later became a noted football coach. Name him.

Q17   Who was the only member of the Chicago starting infield not to be implicated in the "Black Sox" scandal?

Q18   The Pale Hose won their first pennant in 40 years with a victory on September 22, 1959. Who did they defeat to clinch the title?

Q19   What two Sox pitchers combined to shut out the Dodgers in Game 1 of the 1959 World Series?

Q20   Though Chicago lost the 1959 World Series 4–2 to the L.A. Dodgers, this South Sider set a Series record for a six-game match with 10 RBIs. Name him.

Q21   After capturing Game 1 of the 1983 AL Championship Series, the Sox lost the next three while recording only one run in 27 innings. Who scored Chicago's lone run?

Q22   Who tossed a five-hitter for Chicago in Game 5 of the 1983 ALCS?

CHICAGO WHITE SOX

A9   It was made into a best-of-nine affair. (The first since 1903.)

A10   Kenesaw Mountain Landis

A11   The Sox were heavily favored to win at first, but eventually became underdogs in the betting odds.

A12
Eddie Cicotte	Chick Gandil
Lefty Williams	Swede Risberg
Joe Jackson	Buck Weaver
Happy Felsch	Fred McMullin

A13   He hit Cincinnati's first batter, Morrie Rath, with a pitch.

A14   Joe Jackson

A15   Lefty Williams

A16   Greasy Neale

A17   Eddie Collins

A18   The Indians, at Cleveland

A19   Early Wynn (seven-plus innings)
Gerry Staley

A20   Ted Kluszewski

A21   Ron Kittle (Game 3; third inning)

A22   LaMarr Hoyt

*** SOX FAST FACTS ***

In the 1906 World Series, the victorious Sox hit only .198 as a team, and the Cubs batted an even less impressive .196.

TRADES, WAIVES, AND ACQUISITIONS

Q1   In 1901, Charles Comiskey raided the Cubs and swiped three prominent members from his team's crosstown rival. Name the trio who came to the Stockings.

Q2   Who did Charles Comiskey purchase at a cost of $50,000 from Connie Mack's Philadelphia A's in 1915?

Q3   Owner J. Louis Comiskey and GM Harry Grabiner purchased three players from Connie Mack and his Philadelphia A's during the 1932 World Series. Who came to Chicagoland for $150,000?

Q4   After little more than three seasons in a Sox uniform, Moose Skowron was traded on May 6, 1967. To what team was the Moose traded in exchange for infielder Charles Nash?

Q5   The Sox acquired Oscar Gamble, LaMarr Hoyt, Bob Polinsky, and cash from the Yankees in exchange for one player. Who was sent packing to the Big Apple in the 1977 deal?

Q6   In acquiring Bobby Bonds from the Angels in 1977, the Sox allowed California to choose one of two players in return. Eventually, Chicago gave up Brian Downing. Who was the other player offered in the deal?

Q7   Name the three pitchers who were sent to San Diego on December 6, 1984, for Ozzie Guillen, Tim Lollar, and Luis Salazar.

Q8   Scott Fletcher is in his second tour of duty with the White Sox. He and Ed Correa were traded to Texas in 1985 for a pair of players, but in 1989 Fletcher returned to Chicagoland. For whom was Fletcher traded in 1985, and who was involved in the 1989 deal?

Q9   Name the Chicago infielder who was given up in the deal that brought Yankee pitcher Ken Patterson to the South Siders.

Q10   Dan Pasqua, Mark Salas, and Steve Rosenberg came to the Sox in a deal for Richard Dotson and Scott Neilsen in 1987. With what team did the Sox trade?

Q11   In an off-season trade with Kansas City, the Sox sent Floyd Bannister and Dave Cochrane to the Royals for four players. Who came to Chicago in the deal?

Q12   Who did Chicago acquire when they sent Harold Baines and Fred Manrique to the Texas Rangers?

CHICAGO WHITE SOX

A1   Jimmy Callahan
Sandow Mertes
Clark Griffith

A2   Eddie Collins

A3   Al Simmons
Jimmy Dykes
Mule Haas

A4   The California Angels

A5   Bucky Dent

A6   Jim Essian

A7   LaMarr Hoyt
Todd Simmons
Kevin Kristan

A8   In 1985, Fletcher went to Texas for Wayne Tolleson and Dave Schmidt. He returned to the White Sox from the Rangers in 1989 in the Harold Baines deal.

A9   Jerry Royster (The deal also involved minor leaguer Mike Soper, going to New York for pitcher Jeff Pries.)

A10   The Yankees

A11   John Davis
Greg Hibbard
Chuck Mount
Melido Perez

A12   Sammy Sosa
Scott Fletcher
Wilson Alvarez

TRADES, WAIVES, AND ACQUISITIONS

Q13   Name the two pitchers who were swapped between the Sox and the Cubs on December 22, 1989.

Q14   Experience was sacrificed for youth as the Sox traded veteran Jerry Reuss to Milwaukee in 1989 for this promising pitcher. Who joined the Sox?

Q15   Who came to Chicagoland in exchange for Eric King and Shawn Hillegas in a 1990 trade with Cleveland?

Q16   Veteran Tim Raines and two minor league pitchers came to the Sox in a 1991 swap with the Montreal Expos. Name the pair of players who were sent north of the border.

Q17   The Sox picked up Pete Rose, Jr., in a trade for minor leaguer Joe Borowski in the spring of 1991. In whose system was Rose playing?

Q18   At the end of spring training 1991, the Sox were wheeling and dealing with the Padres. Name the two players who came to the South Siders in exchange for Adam Peterson and Steve Rosenberg.

Q19   How many first-round draft choices were on the 1991 edition of the White Sox?

Q20   In an early-1992 transaction, the Sox sent minor leaguers Domingo Jean and Robert Wickman to the Big Apple as part of the Steve Sax deal. What major leaguer was also traded to the Yanks?

CHICAGO WHITE SOX

A13   Rich Scheid went to the Sox for Chuck Mount.

A14   Brian Drahman

A15   Cory Snyder

A16   Ivan Calderon
Barry Jones

A17   The Baltimore Orioles'

A18   Warren Newson
Joey Cora

A19   18

A20   Melido Perez

*** SOX FAST FACTS ***

WHITE SOX PLAYERS INDUCTED INTO THE HALL OF FAME

Eddie Collins (1939)	Red Faber (1964)
Ed Walsh (1946)	Luke Appling (1964)
Clark Griffith (1946)	John "Jocko" Conlan (1967)
Johnny Evers (1946)	Charles "Red" Ruffing (1967)
Al Simmons (1953)	Harry Hooper (1971)
Albert "Chief" Bender (1953)	Early Wynn (1972)
Ray Schalk (1955)	George Kell (1983)
Ted Lyons (1955)	Luis Aparicio (1984)
Eddie Roush (1962)	Hoyt Wilhelm (1985)

Chicago Bulls

THE SUITS

Q1 Who was the Bulls' founder and first owner when the team debuted in 1966?

Q2 Jerry Reinsdorf purchased a controlling interest in another sports franchise in 1981. Name the team.

Q3 Name the two Chicago skippers who have earned Coach of the Year honors.

Q4 What Bull bench boss has the dubious distinction of being nailed with three technical fouls in one game?

Q5 Dick Motta was at the Bulls' helm for 656 regular-season games and 47 postseason contests—the longest tenure of any Chicago head coach. Who was at the helm for the shortest term?

Q6 Johnny Kerr moved from the playing court to the bench when he became the Bulls' head coach. For what team did he play in the 1965–66 season?

Q7 What NBA record did Johnny Kerr establish during his playing career?

Q8 Johnny Kerr returned to the Bulls in 1973 as a business manager. For what NBA team (besides Chicago) did Kerr hold the head coaching position?

Q9 At what Big Sky Conference school did Dick Motta coach before he became the Bulls' second bench boss in 1968–69?

Q10 What team attempted to lure Dick Motta to the ABA in the early 1970s?

Q11 Dick Motta was dismissed after the 1975–76 season when the team took a dramatic dive from the previous year. How many fewer games than the year before did Chicago win in Motta's final season?

CHICAGO BULLS

A1   Dick Klein

A2   The Chicago White Sox

A3   Johnny Kerr (1967)
Dick Motta (1971)

A4   Dick Motta (Bulls vs. Seattle; February 2, 1971)

A5   Scotty Robertson (1979: 11–15)

A6   The Baltimore Bullets

A7   Consecutive games played (917)

A8   The Phoenix Suns

A9   Weber State (in Utah)

A10   The Dallas Chaparrals

A11   23 games (1974–75: 47–35; 1975–76: 24–58)

A12   Phil Johnson (1971–72 through 1973–74, under Dick Motta)

THE SUITS

Q12 Who was the Bulls' first assistant coach?

Q13 Prior to becoming head coach in 1976, Ed Badger was a Bull assistant. At the same time, he held the post of athletic director and basketball skipper at a local college. At what school did he moonlight?

Q14 The second player taken in the 1963 draft became the youngest general manager in the NBA when he joined the Bulls' front office in 1978. Who is he?

Q15 When Larry Costello came to Chicago, he sported two NBA championship rings. With what teams did he earn his jewelry?

Q16 Scotty Robinson was named interim coach of the Bulls in February 1979. Name the deposed skipper he replaced and the coach who succeeded Robertson.

Q17 Scotty Robertson had coaching experience before coming to Chicagoland. Where did he serve his apprenticeship?

Q18 Identify the three men who coached the Bulls during the 1981–82 season.

Q19 Paul Westhead was at the Lakers' helm before coming to the Bulls for a single season (1982–83). What was unique about his dismissal from the L.A. organization?

Q20 Kevin Loughery became the seventh coach in team history in 1983. What three franchises had he piloted previously?

Q21 Doug Collins was the first overall pick in the 1973 draft. What college did he attend?

Q22 Collins's 1987–88 team was the first Bull club to have better than a .500 record since when?

Q23 As an 18-year-old, Phil Jackson played baseball with the Williston Headliners and was a hot pro prospect. What Hall of Famer pitched against Jackson in a 1963 exhibition game?

Q24 For what now-veteran NBA coach did All-American Phil Jackson play at the University of North Dakota?

Q25 Phil Jackson's team won the Continental Basketball Association's title in 1984, and he was named that league's Coach of the Year a season later. What club was he coaching at the time?

CHICAGO BULLS

A13   Wright College

A14   Rod Thorn

A15   Player: Philadelphia 76ers (1966–67)
Coach: Milwaukee Bucks (1970–71)

A16   Larry Costello was fired and replaced temporarily by Robertson. Jerry Sloan was named head coach shortly thereafter.

A17   He was the first coach of the New Orleans Jazz. (His tenure lasted 14 games—which included 13 defeats.)

A18   Jerry Sloan
Phil Johnson
Rod Thorn

A19   It came while the Lakers were in the midst of a five-game win streak.

A20   Philadelphia 76ers (1972–73)
New York/New Jersey Nets (1973–74 through 1980–81)
Atlanta Hawks (1981–82 through 1982–83)

A21   Illinois State University

A22   1980–81 (.549)

A23   Satchel Paige (Jackson got a hit off Paige while the pitcher was on a barnstorming tour of the country.)

A24   Bill Fitch

A25   The Albany Patroons

THE SUITS

Q26 Phil Jackson got off on the right foot in his first season as the Bulls' coach when he posted a 55–27 record. Whose team-best mark of 44–38 did he surpass?

Q27 Jackson put his name in the record books as the coach with the best career winning percentage in the playoffs—25–8, for a .751 mark. Whose record of .685 did he surpass?

Q28 Though he led his team to the NBA Championship, Phil Jackson received only four votes in balloting for the 1991 Coach of the Year. Who won the award?

THE UNIFORMS

Q1 What Bull was the first player in NBA history to score a quadruple double in a game?

Q2 Michael Jordan holds the club record for election to the All-Star Game. Who is second with four selections?

Q3 Name the two Bulls who were selected to the West All-Star team in 1967.

Q4 Who won the NBA's All-Star three-point shootout in 1990?

Q5 Who was the first Bull elected to the NBA All-Rookie team?

Q6 What 10-year veteran is the only player to have his number retired by the Bulls?

Q7 Who was the only Bull to don uniform No. 0?

Q8 Who is the only Bull to score 56 points in a game besides Michael Jordan?

Q9 Who was the last Bull before Michael Jordan to lead the team in scoring for the season?

Q10 What Bull set a Big Eight record by shooting 62 percent in his collegiate career?

Q11 Only two Chicago players have led the NBA in field goal percentage. Name them.

CHICAGO BULLS

A26   Ed Badger's (1976–77)

A27   Pat Riley's (102–47)

A28   Houston's Don Chaney

A1   Nate Thurmond (October 18, 1974: vs. Atlanta—22 points, 14 rebounds, 13 assists, 12 blocked shots)

A2   Chet Walker (1970, 1971, 1973, 1974)

A3   Guy Rodgers
Jerry Sloan

A4   Craig Hodges

A5   Erwin Mueller (1966–67)

A6   Jerry Sloan (1966–76)

A7   Orlando Woolridge (1981–86)

A8   Chet Walker (February 6, 1972: vs. Cincinnati)

A9   Orlando Woolridge (1985–86: 1,448 points)

A10   Kansas's Mark Randall

A11   Walt Bellamy (1961–62: .519)
Artis Gilmore (1980–81: .670; 1981–82: .652)

Q3 (Trades, Waives, and Acquisitions). This player was the Bulls' first ever draft pick. Name him.

CHICAGO BULLS

Q13 (Trades, Waives, and Acquisitions). Identify the man in the middle who came to Chicago for Cliff Ray, a first round draft pick, and cash in a 1974 swap with Golden State.

Q12 Name the Chicago player who has led the NBA in free throw percentage.

Q13 Name the five Bull starters in the team's inaugural season.

Q14 Who was the last player from the Bulls' first season to leave the team?

Q15 Who was the only Bull to play in all 81 games of the franchise's first season?

Q16 Identify the Bull who set a league record for assists in the franchise's debut season (1966–67).

Q17 From what club was Jerry Sloan acquired in the 1966 expansion draft?

Q18 What was Jerry Sloan's nickname?

Q19 At the time of his retirement, Jerry Sloan was the third-best rebounding guard in NBA history (5,615). Who was ahead of him in the record books?

Q20 Name the two seven-foot players who shared the center position on the 1968–69 team.

Q21 How many consecutive seasons did Bob Love lead the Bulls in scoring?

Q22 This present-day NBA coach came to the Bulls in a trade with Portland in 1973. Who is this former guard?

Q23 What was the name of the soul-food restaurant Nate Thurmond owned in San Francisco?

Q24 Name the Bull troika who played on the 1976 gold medal U.S. Olympic team.

Q25 Artis Gilmore was the Bulls' first pick in the 1976 Dispersal Draft of ABA players. With what ABA team did Gilmore play?

Q26 What accolade did Artis Gilmore receive in 1981?

Q27 The Supersonics' first-round pick in 1970, this center opted for the ABA and played four seasons with the New York Nets. He returned to the NBA in 1974 when he signed with the Celtics, and he joined the Bulls in 1977 as a free agent. Name the pivot.

Q28 Identify the Bulls' 1978 first-round draftee who placed second in the Rookie of the Year derby.

CHICAGO BULLS

A12 Chet Walker (1970–71: .859)

A13 Center Len Chappell, forwards Don Kojis and Bob Boozer, and guards
Guy Rodgers and Jerry Sloan

A14 Jerry Sloan (1966–67 through 1975–76)

A15 Guy Rodgers

A16 Guy Rodgers (908 assists—11.2 per game)

A17 The Baltimore Bullets

A18 "Spider"

A19 Oscar Robertson (7,804)
Hal Greer (5,665)

A20 Tom Boerwinkle
Dave Newmark

A21 Seven (1969–70 through 1975–76)

A22 Rick Adelman

A23 The Beginning

A24 Scott May
Tate Armstrong
Steve Sheppard

A25 The Kentucky Colonels

A26 He was named the NBA's all-time field goal percentage leader (.577).

A27 Jim Ard

A28 Reggie Theus (K.C.'s Phil Ford won the award.)

Q29   This free agent guard was picked up in 1979 after he was released by the Bucks to make room for Norm Van Lier. Name the backcourter.

Q30   David Greenwood was only the third UCLA player to earn first-team all-league (Pac-10) honors three times. Who were the first two Bruins so honored?

Q31   Name the Bull who ordered a hot dog, popcorn, and soda while sitting on the bench during a 1981 game.

Q32   Orlando Woolridge's cousin also saw action in the NBA. Who is he?

Q33   Two centers were drafted ahead of Michael Jordan in the 1984 draft. Name the pair of pivots and the school each attended.

Q34   Who wore No. 23 before Michael Jordan made the digits famous?

Q35   Who was Michael Jordan's backcourt mate when the Air-atola debuted with the Bulls in 1984?

Q36   In his freshman season, Jordan became only the third player in NBA history to lead his club in rebounds, assists, steals, and points. Who were the first two pacesetters?

Q37   Where did Michael Jordan break his foot on October 29, 1985—the third game of the season?

Q38   Who was the last player, before Michael Jordan started monopolizing it, to win the league's annual scoring title?

Q39   Only two men have ever made more free throws in a game than Sir Michael (February 26, 1987: vs. New Jersey—26/27). Who had better numbers from the charity stripe?

Q40   Only one Bull other than Michael Jordan led the team in scoring in a game during the 1987–88 season. Name him.

Q41   Another milestone in Jordan's phenomenal career occurred in the 1988 playoffs, when he scored 50 or more points in consecutive games. Against what team did he singe the nets and thereby become the first player to perform that feat in the postseason?

Q42   Only three players have ever amassed 2,000-plus points, 600-plus rebounds, and 600-plus assists in a single season. Jordan did it in 1989. Who are the other two super-hoopsters?

CHICAGO BULLS

A29 Delmer Beshore

A30 Lew Alcindor
Bill Walton

A31 Quintin Dailey

A32 Willis Reed

A33 Hakeem Olajuwon—University of Houston
Sam Bowie—University of Kentucky

A34 Mike Bratz

A35 Ennis Whatley

A36 Dave Cowens (1977–78)
Larry Bird (1982–83)

A37 Golden State's Oakland Coliseum Arena

A38 Atlanta's Dominique Wilkins (1985–86: 30.3 points/game)

A39 Adrian Dantley (January 4, 1984: 28/29; November 25, 1983: 27/31)
Wilt Chamberlain (March 2, 1962: 28/32)

A40 John Paxson (On December 1, 1987, against Golden State, Paxson had
19 points to Jordan's 16.)

A41 The Cleveland Cavaliers

A42 John Havlicek (1971–72)
Oscar Robertson (1961–62; 1962–63; 1963–64; 1964–65)

Q43   It ranks as one of the most memorable shots in Bull history: Michael Jordan pops a buzzer-beating jumper for a 101–100 win over the Cavs in the final game of the first round of the 1989 playoffs. What Cleveland player was guarding His Highness?

Q44   On February 14, 1990, Michael Jordan wore another number for a game against the Orlando Magic. What number did Sir Michael sport?

Q45   The Cleveland Coliseum was the setting on March 28, 1990, when Michael Jordan hit the hole for 69 points. Who was the only other Bull to score in double figures that night?

Q46   Who are the only players to score more points in a game than Jordan (69 points: March 28, 1990)?

Q47   Whose record did Jordan break when after five seasons he became the team's all-time leading scorer in 1989–90?

Q48   Against what team did Jordan score his 15,000th career point on January 9, 1991?

Q49   In the fourth quarter of Game 2 of the NBA Finals, Michael Jordan made THE MOVE. While driving for a dunk, he eyed a defender and, at the top of his flight, lowered his body and changed hands with the ball before finally banking it in. Who was defending him on the play?

Q50   Jordan's air show in the 1991 five-game championship series resulted in two new league records. Sir Michael set five game standards for assists and steals. Whose records did he break?

Q51   Of the 99 games played by Chicago during the 1991 regular and postseason, how many times did Michael Jordan lead the club in scoring?

Q52   Jordan's career playoff scoring average stands at 34.6 points after the 1991 postseason, tops in the history of the NBA. Who is second in that category?

Q53   Besides Michael Jordan, what three players have won an NBA scoring title and the championship in the same year?

Q54   What was unique about Michael Jordan's appearance on the June 24, 1991, cover of *Sports Illustrated*?

Q55   Horace Grant is one of two players in Clemson history with over 1,500 points, 500 rebounds, and 200 assists. Who is the other?

CHICAGO BULLS

A43 Craig Ehlo

A44 12 (His jersey had been stolen. To make matters worse, the Bulls lost the game, 135–129, in OT.)

A45 Horace Grant (who had 16 points in the 117–113 win)

A46 Wilt Chamberlain (six times)
David Thompson (April 9, 1978: 73 points)
Elgin Baylor (November 15, 1960: 71 points)

A47 Bob Love's (In seven years with the Bulls, Love notched 12,623 points.)

A48 The Philadelphia 76ers

A49 Sam Perkins

A50 Assists: Jordan broke Bob Cousy's mark (57, to Cousy's 53 in 1961).
Steals: Jordan broke Terry Porter's record (14, to Porter's 10 in 1990).

A51 92 (Of the remaining seven, Paxson led in one, Grant did the same, Pippen led in four, and Grant and Pippen were tied for the lead in one.)

A52 Jerry West (West averaged 29.1 points per playoff game.)

A53 Kareem Abdul-Jabbar (1971)
George Mikan (1949, 1950)
Joe Fulks (1947)

A54 Jordan's appearance marked the first time in the magazine's history that the same person was on the cover four straight times. (The fourth cover was an inset shot.)

A55 Vincent Hamilton (1980–85)

THE UNIFORMS

Q56 Charles Oakley's 18 offensive rebounds in a game was the third-highest total recorded in the NBA during the 1985-86 season. Who is the only player to have bettered the mark?

Q57 Charles Oakley finished the 1987–88 season with 936 rebounds, second best in the league. Who edged out Oakley for the crown by two boards?

Q58 Bill Cartwright scored his 10,000th career point on November 4, 1989. Who was Chicago playing that evening?

Q59 Name the Bull whose middle name is MacBeth.

Q60 Horace and Harvey Grant are one of two sets of twins to have played in the NBA. Identify the other twosome.

Q61 Calling him a "soldier gone AWOL," coach Phil Jackson suspended Stacey King for one game during the latter part of the 1990–91 season. Before King, who was the last player suspended from the team for the same infraction?

Q62 Mark Randall's coach at Kansas was the same man who recruited Michael Jordan at North Carolina. Who is he?

Q63 Forward Mark Randall was a medical redshirt during Kansas's 1987–88 NCAA Championship season. What malady qualified Randall for a spot on the sick list?

SETTING THE STANDARD

Q1 What league record did the Bulls establish in their inaugural season?

Q2 Who did the Bulls tip off against when they set a team record for the largest hometown crowd (21,652) on April 8, 1977?

Q3 The longest (2:40) and shortest (1:32) regulation games in team history were against the same opponent. Who was Chicago's competition?

Q4 The fewest number of points scored by the Bulls occurred in a road game on March 6, 1976, against Phoenix. What was Chicago held to that day?

Q5 The Bulls were on a roll in 1973 when they won 12 straight games from October 13 to November 11. What team halted the streak on November 13?

CHICAGO BULLS

A56   Moses Malone, with 21 and 19. (The stat has been kept since 1973.)

A57   Michael Cage of the Clippers (Cage pulled down 30 rebounds in his last game to capture the title.)

A58   The Boston Celtics

A59   John Paxson

A60   Tom and Dick van Arsdale

A61   Orlando Woolridge (during the 1985–86 season)

A62   Roy Williams

A63   He had surgery for jaw realignment.

———————————— · ————————————

A1   Most wins (33) by an expansion team

A2   The Houston Rockets (Chicago won, 113–109.)

A3   The Houston Rockets (The longest was on November 29, 1983, and the Bulls lost, 116–110. The shortest was on December 2, 1978, and Chicago prevailed, 105–91.)

A4   65 points (The Suns won, 88–65.)

A5   The Phoenix Suns (116–108)

SETTING THE STANDARD

Q6 Name the sharpshooter who holds a record for consecutive field goals made (14) by an opposing player against the Bulls in one game.

Q7 Name the hoopster who started in 10 consecutive Opening Day lineups, the most ever by a Bull player.

Q8 Kyle Macy and Gene Banks tied each other in this category while setting a team record during the 1985–86 campaign. In what category did the tandem excel?

Q9 Who is the only player to score more points in a rookie season than Walt Bellamy (1961–62: 2,495)?

Q10 Three Bulls set a Chicago record when they combined to hit on six consecutive three-point shots. Name the trio who scored 18 points in 1:29.

Q11 Who sank 11 consecutive baskets and established a Chicago record against archrival Detroit?

Q12 The 1969 season ended on a dismal note when Chicago gave up 158 points in the final game, the most a Bull team had ever given up. What club set a record for most points and field goals (67) against the Bulls in a single game?

Q13 The longest shot ever made by a Bull was an 84-footer against the Spurs. Who sank the "Hail Mary"?

Q14 Against what now-defunct team did Bill Cartwright match an NBA record for most free throws (19 for 19) without a miss?

Q15 What Bull holds a team record for single-season free throw percentage?

Q16 This Bull set a team record by pulling down 37 rebounds in a 1970 game against Phoenix. Who was this chairman of the boards?

Q17 Identify the player who set a franchise standard with 24 assists in a single game.

Q18 What durable forward established a team mark when he averaged 43 minutes per game in 1970–71?

Q19 What Bull set both a team and league record when he was tagged with six personal fouls in one quarter?

Q20 What team record do Sam Smith, Kyle Macy, and Craig Hodges share?

CHICAGO BULLS

A6   Washington's Greg Ballard (4/9/83: at Washington)

A7   Jerry Sloan

A8   Most steals in a season (81)

A9   Wilt Chamberlain (1959–60: 2,707)

A10 Rod Higgins (one)
Reggie Theus (three)
Quintin Dailey (two)
(November 13, 1982: at Indiana. Chicago lost, 119–115.)

A11 Clem Haskins (February 15, 1970; at Detroit)

A12 The Detroit Pistons (March 23, 1969. Chicago fell, 158–114.)

A13 Norm Van Lier (January 19, 1977; at San Antonio)

A14 Kansas City (November 7, 1981)

A15 Ricky Sobers (1980–81: .935)

A16 Tom Boerwinkle

A17 Guy Rodgers (December 21, 1968; vs. the Knicks)

A18 Bob Love

A19 Michael Jordan (January 31, 1989; in the fourth quarter vs. Detroit)

A20 Each of them has made four-point plays.
(Smith: at Milwaukee on October 21, 1979;
Macy: at Indiana on November 19, 1985;
Hodges: at Seattle on March 25, 1989)

Q21 In what category did John Paxson top all NBA guards during the 1990–91 regular season?

Q22 What opposing player once attempted 50 field goals against the Bulls, setting a Stadium record?

Q23 What Bull holds a club record for overtime points with 13?

FYI

Q1 Name the three pro basketball franchises that called Chicago home before the Bulls were born in 1966.

Q2 In what season were the Bulls moved from the Midwest to the Eastern Conference?

Q3 The Bulls won the first regular-season game they ever played. Who did they defeat?

Q4 Where did the Bulls call home in their inaugural season?

Q5 The first home game for the Bulls was a 119–116 win on October 18, 1966. Who did Chicago eke out a victory against before its first home crowd?

Q6 The Bulls played before the smallest hometown crowd (891) in franchise history on November 7, 1968. What team did they face that evening?

Q7 Identify the enraged Indiana Pacer who did his best Reggie Roby imitation when he drop-kicked a basketball into the stands of Chicago Stadium on March 23, 1991.

Q8 The Bulls are away from home on Thanksgiving every season. Why?

Q9 Identify the only major league arena that is older than Chicago Stadium.

Q10 The Bulls compiled a 67–15 record in 1991–92. Only three teams have ever had better seasons. Name the three franchises.

CHICAGO BULLS

A21 Best field goal percentage (.548)

A22 Rick Barry (February 5, 1967. San Francisco won in overtime, 142–141.)

A23 Michael Jordan (March 30, 1990; vs. New York)

---·---

A1 The R.I.P. Stags (1946–50)
The Packers (1961–62)
The Zephyrs (1962–63)

A2 1980–81

A3 The St. Louis Hawks (October 15, 1966: 104–97 at St. Louis)

A4 The International Amphitheater

A5 The San Francisco Warriors

A6 The Seattle Supersonics

A7 Chuck Person (He was fined $2,500.)

A8 The circus is at the Stadium every year at that time.

A9 Boston Garden

A10 L.A. Lakers (1971–72: 69–13)
Philadelphia 76ers (1966–67: 68–13)
Boston Celtics (1972–73: 68–14)

GLORY DAYS

Q1 How many times has Chicago won a seven-game playoff series?

Q2 What team has Chicago defeated the most times in the playoffs?

Q3 How many times has Chicago lost a seven-game playoff series?

Q4 How many times have the Bulls been eliminated from the playoffs by the eventual NBA champion?

Q5 What team has defeated Chicago in every playoff game in which the two teams have participated?

Q6 What club has eliminated the Bulls four times in the NBA playoffs—the most of any team?

Q7 Chicago qualified for the 1966–67 playoffs in its inaugural season when it finished fourth in the five-team Western Division. What club did the Bulls beat out in the division standings?

Q8 The 1966–67 Bulls made it to the playoffs in their debut season, only to be eliminated in the first round, 3–0. Who swept Chicago that season?

Q9 The Bulls' first-ever playoff win took place on March 27, 1968. What team fell victim to Chicago that night?

Q10 What Bull hit the hole for 41 points in the just-cited game?

Q11 The Hawks eliminated the Bulls from postseason play in 1970. The lone bright spot occurred in Game 4, when the Bulls romped, 131–120. Who had 13 assists to lead Chicago?

Q12 Over what team did the Bulls register back-to-back victories to launch them into the 1971 playoffs?

Q13 Against what team did Chicago win its first playoff series?

Q14 Who was the only Bull to play on both the 1981 and 1985 playoff teams?

Q15 The Bulls began a fashion tradition for the playoffs in 1989 that symbolized team unity. What did they do to show their togetherness?

Q16 The Bulls' Phil Jackson and L.A.'s Mike Dunleavy both made their first coaching appearances in the NBA Finals in 1991. When was the last time both coaches had no previous experience in the Championship Series?

Q17 With what name did assistant coach John Bach christen the Bulls' tenacious defensive squad in the 1991 title match against the Lakers?

CHICAGO BULLS

A1   Twice (1973–74; vs. Detroit—Western Semifinals
         (1991–92: vs. New York—Eastern Finals)

A2   New York (four times—1981: 2–0
                          1989: 4–2
                          1991: 3–0
                          1992: 4–3)

A3   Four times (L.A.—Western Semifinals 1970–71;
                 L.A.—Western Semifinals 1972–73;
                 Golden State—Western Semifinals 1974–75;
                 Detroit—Eastern Finals 1989–90)

A4   Seven times (1971–72—L.A.; 1974–75—Golden State; 1976–77—
Portland; 1980–81—Boston; 1985–86—Boston; 1988–89, 1989–90—
Detroit)

A5   The Boston Celtics (1980–81: Eastern Semifinals—0–4; 1985–86:
Eastern, First Round—0–3; 1986–87: Eastern, First Round—0–3)

A6   Los Angeles (1968: 4–1; 1971: 4–3; 1972: 4–0; 1973: 4–3)

A7   The Detroit Pistons

A8   The St. Louis Hawks

A9   The Lakers (104–98. Chicago lost the Western Division Semifinals, 4–1.)

A10   Flynn Robinson

A11   Clem Haskins

A12   The Phoenix Suns (March 12, 1971: 116–92; March 13, 1971: 111–99)

A13   The Detroit Pistons (1974: first round, 4–3)

A14   David Greenwood

A15   The Bulls switched from white to black sneakers for the playoffs.

A16   1981 (Boston's Bill Fitch vs. Houston's Del Harris)

A17   The "Doberman Defense"

Q18 The Bull-Laker matchup in the 1991 finals marked only the second time that teams from the nation's second- and third-largest cities have met in championship competition. What was the only other Chicago-L.A. title match?

Q19 The Bulls' victory in the 1991 NBA Finals made Chicago one of four U.S. cities to win an NBA crown, a World Series, a Stanley Cup, and an NFL Championship. What other cities can boast of the same accomplishment?

Q20 For games 1 and 2 of the 1992 NBA Championship Finals, coach Phil Jackson wore ties which were hand painted by an international celebrity. Who designed the coach's cravats?

Q21 The Bulls made it two in a row in 1992. What Chicago team was the last to win back-to-back championships in any professional sport?

Q22 When the Bulls won three consecutive games at the Forum en route to the 1991 NBA Championship, they tied a league record for three wins on an opponent's floor. Whose mark did they match?

Q23 When the Bulls won the 1990–91 NBA crown, they became the third consecutive club to capture the title on the road. Name the other two teams and the cities in which they emerged victorious.

Q24 Name the three Tar Heels from the 1982 NCAA Championship club who played in the 1991 NBA Finals.

Q25 In the question just cited, name the two Tar Heels starters who are not currently playing pro basketball.

Q26 The Bulls won their first NBA crown with Bill Cartwright averaging 9.6 points per game. Who was the last middle man to earn the title with fewer than 10 points a game?

Q27 Michael Jordan led the Bulls in four of the five playoff games against the Lakers in the 1991 Finals. Who led the club in the other matchup?

CHICAGO BULLS

A18   The White Sox—Dodger World Series of 1959, in which the Dodgers prevailed.

A19   New York
Philadelphia
Detroit

A20   Jerry Garcia (The Grateful Dead's guitarist and vocalist)

A21   The Chicago Bears (1940 and 1941)

A22   The Detroit Pistons' (1989–90 playoffs)

A23   Both titles were won by Detroit. In 1990, the Pistons clinched the crown at Portland; they took the championship in 1989 at the Forum in L.A.

A24   Chicago: Michael Jordan
L.A.: James Worthy and Sam Perkins

A25   Jimmy Black
Matt Boherty

A26   Wes Unseld of Washington (7.6 points per game)

A27   Scottie Pippen (Game 5: 32 points to Jordan's 30)

***   BULL FAST FACTS   ***

During the 1986–87 season, Michael Jordan became the first Bull to be selected to the first-team All-NBA squad.

Q28 For each category, choose whether Jordan or Magic Johnson held the edge for the 1991 finals.
(A) Minutes Played (228 vs. 220)
(B) Points (156 vs. 93)
(C) 3-Point Baskets (4 vs. 2)
(D) Free Throw Percentage (.951 vs. .848)
(E) Rebounds (40 vs. 33)
(F) Assists (62 vs. 57)
(G) Steals (14 vs. 6)
(H) Blocked Shots (7 vs. 0)
(I) Personal Fouls (18 vs. 10)
(J) Turnovers (22 vs. 18)

Q29 The Bulls won the 1992 NBA Championship on their home court. What was the last pro sports league title captured in Chicago?

Q30 Who was the only member of the 1992 NBA Champion Bulls to have not played for the 1991 championship club?

Q31 In the first game of the 1992 Bulls-Blazers finals, Michael Jordan went to the hole for 35 points in the first half. Whose record did "His Airness" break for points in one half?

Q32 How many three pointers did Jordan hit in that extraordinary performance of the first half?

Q33 The Bulls entered the fourth quarter of Game 6 of the 1992 NBA Championship 15 points behind the Portland Trail Blazers (79–64). Whose three-point basket at the beginning of that period started a 14–2 run for Chicago?

Q34 By rebounding from 15 points down at the start of the fourth quarter in Game 6, the Bulls set an NBA playoff record. What club held the previous record?

Q35 Michael Jordan won both the NBA regular season and Finals MVP in consecutive seasons—1991 and 1992. While he is the only player to win both awards in consecutive seasons, one other cager has captured the dual awards twice. Who is he?

Q36 The Chicago Bulls became the third consecutive repeat NBA Champions in 1992, but only the fifth franchise in NBA history to repeat. Name the previous repeaters.

CHICAGO BULLS

A28 Jordan—B, G, H, I
Magic—A, C, D, E, F, J

A29 The Bears' 1963 NFL title.

A30 Bobby Hansen

A31 Elgin Baylor's (Baylor notched 33 points in 1962.)

A32 Six (which set another NBA playoff record)

A33 Bobby Hansen's

A34 San Francisco (April 23, 1967: vs. Philadelphia; 12 points)

A35 Larry Bird (1984 and 1986)

A36 Minneapolis Lakers (1949 and 1950; 1952, '53, '54)
Boston Celtics (1959 through 1966; 1968 and 1969)
Los Angeles Lakers (1987 and 1988)
Detroit Pistons (1989 and 1990)

*** BULL FAST FACTS ***

ACCURATE ARTIS—
Artis Gilmore holds the NBA record for field goal percentage
(minimum: 2,000 field goals made) with a .599 percentage (9,570
attempted, 5,732 made). Second to Gilmore is James Donaldson
with a .587 percentage.

TRADES, WAIVES, AND ACQUISITIONS

Q1   Who was the first Notre Dame graduate drafted by the Bulls?

Q2   Who was the first "hardship" selection in Bull history?

Q3   Who was the Bulls' first-ever draft pick?

Q4   Who was the first player selected by the Bulls in the 1966 expansion draft?

Q5   This guard was the Bulls' first bona fide star and was acquired in 1966 from the Warriors for Jim King, Jeff Mullins, a draft choice, and cash. Who was this early-day player?

Q6   Early in the 1967–68 campaign, the cash-strapped Bulls traded Guy Rodgers to Cincinnati for money, two draft choices, and this player. Who came to the Bulls in the deal?

Q7   In one of the best trades for the Bulls ever, the team shipped Flynn Robinson to Milwaukee for two of that franchise's best-known players. Name the tandem that came to Chicagoland in the 1968 deal. (Hint: They share the same first name.)

Q8   The Bulls traded Barry Clemens and Bob Boozer, the 1968–69 team scoring champ, to Seattle in 1969. Who did they receive in return?

Q9   The Bulls sent Jim Fox and a draft choice to Cincinnati in late 1971 for a draft choice and this playmaker. Name the guard who came to Chicago in the deal.

Q10   Starting guard Matt Guokas left Chicago for the first time in 1971. Who was acquired from Cincinnati when Guokas went to the Royals?

Q11   The Bulls' 1972 first-round draft pick never played for Chicago. Who was he?

Q12   What Princeton grad came to the Bulls in return for Kevin Kunnert and Gar Heard in a 1973 trade with the Buffalo Braves?

Q13   Identify the man in the middle who came to Chicago for Cliff Ray, a first-round draft pick, and cash in a 1974 swap with Golden State.

Q14   The popular Bob Weiss was sent packing in 1974 to the Buffalo Braves. Who made his return to the Windy City from the Queen City?

Q15   Who did the Bulls acquire after they dished out a cool million in the ABA dispersal draft in 1976?

CHICAGO BULLS

A1   Orlando Woolridge (first-round pick in 1981)

A2   Cliff Pondexter (1974: No. 1 draft choice)

A3   Dave Schellhase of Purdue (10th overall pick in 1966)

A4   Jerry Sloan

A5   Guy Rodgers

A6   Flynn Robinson

A7   Bob Love
Bob Weiss

A8   Bob Kauffman

A9   Norm Van Lier

A10   Charlie Paulk

A11   Michigan State's Ralph Simpson (He was already playing with the ABA's Denver Nuggets.)

A12   John Hummer

A13   Nate Thurmond

A14   Matt Guokas

A15   Artis Gilmore

TRADES, WAIVES, AND ACQUISITIONS

Q16 The Bulls paid a high price for this former Brave. He was acquired from Buffalo in exchange for a first-round draft pick, but lasted just one and a half seasons before retiring in 1977. Name him.

Q17 No Magic was involved for the Bulls in the 1979 draft. In a fateful flip of a coin, the team lost an opportunity to take Earvin Johnson in the draft. Whom did they select instead?

Q18 The Bulls lost Mickey Johnson through free agency to the Indiana Pacers in 1979. Whom did Chicago receive in return?

Q19 The Bulls and Trail Blazers had the fourth and 10th picks, respectively, in the 1980 draft. Each of the teams selected a player and then swapped them for each other. Who was involved in the unique trade?

Q20 Who was sent packing to the Lone Star State in 1982 when the Bulls acquired Mark Olberding and Dave Corzine from San Antonio?

Q21 What first-round pick did the acquisition of Caldwell Jones cost the Bulls?

Q22 To what now-defunct team did the Bulls send Reggie Theus for Steve Johnson and a draft pick in the 1984–85 season?

Q23 No. 1 pick Keith Lee and guard Ennis Whatley were dispatched to Cleveland in the summer of 1985. What pair of players came to the Bulls in return?

Q24 What frontcourt player did Chicago trade to San Antonio for George Gervin in a 1985 transaction?

Q25 Early in the 1986–87 season, the Knicks traded their top draft pick to Seattle for Gerald Henderson. The Sonics had a prearranged deal to send that choice to the Bulls. Whom did Chicago select with the pick?

Q26 Who was the Bulls' second first-round draft pick in the 1987 draft?

Q27 What former Bull was given up in a trade in June 1988 so that Chicago could acquire the services of Bill Cartwright from the Knicks?

Q28 Name the three players who were selected in the first round of the 1989 draft by Chicago.

Q29 Name the 6-foot-10 Yugoslavian guard whom the Bulls pursued for a year but who instead signed a $4 million contract with an Italian team in the summer of 1991.

Q30 Who did the Bulls dispatch to the Sacramento Kings in exchange for Dennis Hopson in a late-1991 deal?

CHICAGO BULLS

A16   Jack Marin

A17   David Greenwood

A18   Ricky Sobers

A19   Portland drafted Iowa's Ronnie Lester, and the Bulls chose Ohio State's Kelvin Ransey. The players were then exchanged; Chicago also gained a future first-round pick.

A20   Artis Gilmore

A21   Mitchell Wiggins

A22   Kansas City

A23   Charles Oakley
Calvin Duncan

A24   David Greenwood

A25   Scottie Pippen (It was the fifth pick in the 1987 lottery.)

A26   Clemson's Horace Grant

A27   Charles Oakley

A28   Stacey King (Oklahoma)
B. J. Armstrong (Iowa)
Jeff Sanders (Georgia Southern)

A29   Toni Kukoc (whom the Bulls selected in the second round of the 1990 draft)

A30   Bobby Hansen (and a second-round draft choice)

Chicago Blackhawks

CHICAGO BLACKHAWKS

Chicago "Black Hawks" ---Stanley Cup Winners, Year 1934

Emblematic of World's Professional Championship

LEFT TO RIGHT — THE LATE CHUCK GARDINER, TOMMY COOK, ROGER JENKINS, LOLA COUTURE, PAUL THOMPSON, JOHNNY GOTTSELIG, LIONEL CONACHER, ART COULTER, TOMMY GORMAN, TAFFY ABEL, DOC ROMNES, LOUIS TRUDELL, JACK LESWICK, MUSH MARSH, JOHNNY McFADDEN, BILL KENDAL, JOE STARK.

THE SUITS

Q1   In 1926, coffee baron Frederick "Major" McLaughlin bought an existing club and moved it to Chicago, where the team became known as the Blackhawks. What was the name of the original franchise?

Q2   Who did Major McLaughlin import to Chicago for the 1927–28 season to teach Blackhawk fans how to yell, shriek, and scream during games?

Q3   Major McLaughlin was married to a world-famous movie star. Who was she?

Q4   After a distinguished 16-year playing career, Hawk VP Bob Pulford was enshrined in the Hockey Hall of Fame in 1991. With what two NHL clubs did the defensive specialist play?

Q5   Name the five general managers in Blackhawk history.

Q6   What general manager's wife designed the Blackhawks' red-black-and-white uniform?

Q7   Name the three Hawk coaches who have led the team to 100 or more points in a season.

Q8   What Chicago skipper had the shortest stint behind the Blackhawk bench?

Q9   In a 1941 game against the Maple Leafs, this Chicago coach pulled goalie Sam LoPresti when his club fell behind and replaced him with an extra forward. Name the Hawk bench boss who was credited with this innovative maneuver.

Q10   This onetime Blackhawk coach, who earned degrees in both math and physical education, played on two Stanley Cup championship teams. Both victories, in 1971 and 1973, were against the Blackhawks. Name the former Chicago bench boss.

CHICAGO BLACKHAWKS

A1   The Portland Rosebuds

A2   McLaughlin brought in a professional jewelry auctioneer from Saskatchewan to coach the fans.

A3   Irene Castle

A4   The Toronto Maple Leafs
The Los Angeles Kings

A5   Frederic McLaughlin (1926–42)
Bill Tobin (1942–54)
Tommy Ivan (1954–77)
Bob Pulford (1977–90)
Mike Keenan (1990–present)
(McLaughlin and Tobin were also owners of the team.)

A6   Tommy Ivan's

A7   Billy Reay (1970–71, 1971–72, 1973–74)
Orval Tessier (1982–83)
Mike Keenan (1990–91)

A8   Pete Muldoon (1926–27)

A9   Paul Thompson (The Hawks lost that game, 3–0, but the tactic has been used ever since.)

A10   Bob Murdoch

*** HAWK FAST FACTS ***

The Blackhawk's first home, the Chicago Coliseum, was built in Europe, but was dismantled and transported stone by stone to the United States. It was originally used as a Union prison during the Civil War.

*** HAWK FAST FACTS ***

Before the Blackhawks moved into Chicago Stadium, the team practiced on the outdoor rink at the Chicago Beach Hotel, since the Coliseum was usually booked for other attractions.

THE SUITS

Q11   In his first three seasons behind the Philadelphia bench, Mike Keenan accomplished something that no other NHL coach had done. What plateau did Keenan reach?

Q12   Mike Keenan reached a career milestone late in the 1990–91 season: He coached his 300th victory in seven seasons as the Hawks knocked off the Rangers, 5–2. Name the only other skippers with 300 wins over seven years.

THE UNIFORMS

Q1   Only three players in Blackhawk history have chalked up 100 points in a season. Name the sharpshooters.

Q2   Name the quartet of Blackhawks who have had their numbers retired by the team.

Q3   Who was the first Chicago native to play for the Blackhawks?

Q4   Who was the first American-born player to notch 30 or more goals in a season for the Blackhawks?

Q5   Who is the first Soviet to play for the Hawks?

Q6   Who was the first Hawk to snare the Selke Trophy as the league's top defensive forward?

Q7   Who was the first Blackhawk chosen to the Campbell Conference All-Star Game since fan balloting began?

Q8   What was Taffy Abel's given name?

Q9   In 1936, Hawk Mike Karakas won the Calder Trophy as the league's top rookie. Two years later, Chicago's Carl Dahlstrom snared the award. Besides winning the same trophy, what else did the two players have in common?

Q10   No sibling rivalry was in evidence on the 1942–43 Blackhawk team when three brothers played for Chicago and even skated on the same line for a short time. Identify the trio.

Q11   By what name was the line of Doug Bentley, Clint Smith, and Bill Mosienko known?

CHICAGO BLACKHAWKS

A11   He became the first skipper in league history to win 40 or more games in each of his first three seasons. (1984–85: 53 wins; 1985–86: 53 victories; 1986–87: 46 wins)

A12   Fred Shero
Glen Sather

--- · ---

A1   Bobby Hull (1968–69)
Denis Savard (five times)
Steve Larmer (1990–1991)

A2   Glenn Hall (No. 1)
Bobby Hull (No. 9)
Stan Mikita (No. 21)
Tony Esposito (No. 35)

A3   Mike O'Connell

A4   Wayne Presley (1986–87)

A5   Igor Kravchuk

A6   Troy Murray (1985–86)

A7   Chris Chelios (1990–91)

A8   Clarence

A9   They were both American-born.

A10   Max Bentley
Doug Bentley
Reggie Bentley

A11   The Pony Line

THE UNIFORMS

Q12 In order for the fans and press to more easily identify the goal scorer, the league initiated a new practice that was introduced in a Blackhawk-Canadien game in 1947. The first player to perform the act was Billy Reay. What trend did he start?

Q13 In an effort to shake up the Hawks in 1947, minor league goaltender Doug Jackson was called up, and the team's regular netminder was demoted. After Jackson surrendered 42 goals in six games, he was exiled to the minors for good, and the regular goalie was brought back. Who was he?

Q14 Who was the first Hawk to have his uniform number retired by the team?

Q15 In a 1951 game against the first-place Red Wings, Hawk goalie Harry Lumley was injured and replaced by Moe Roberts. What position did Roberts hold with the team?

Q16 Against what Hawk goalie did Gordie Howe score his 200th career goal on February 15, 1953?

Q17 The Blackhawks participated in an NHL first when this Montreal goalie wore a face mask in a November 7, 1959, game at the Forum. Who was that masked man?

Q18 What is Chico Maki's given name?

Q19 Who was on the "Million Dollar Line"?

Q20 To what WHA team did Ralph Backstrom and Pat Stapleton defect in 1973?

Q21 What type of apparel did Keith Magnuson regularly go without when he was in uniform?

Q22 What is Keith Magnuson's autobiography entitled?

Q23 Bobby Hull has the honor of being the first Blackhawk to notch 50 goals in a season. Who was the second Chicago skater to achieve the same feat?

Q24 In what sport was Bobby Hull offered a full scholarship from the University of Colorado in 1957?

Q25 In spite of being outscored by Bobby Hull in their rookie seasons, this player edged out the Golden Jet for the Calder Cup. Name this 1957–58 Rookie of the Year.

CHICAGO BLACKHAWKS

A12   Reay was the first player to raise his stick over his head after scoring a goal.

A13   Emile Francis

A14   Stan Mikita (in 1980)

A15   He was the team's trainer. (Chicago won, 6–2. Roberts, who at age 46 was the oldest person to skate in the NHL that year, played 20 minutes of shutout hockey.)

A16   Al Rollins

A17   Jacques Plante

A18   Ronald

A19   Bobby Hull
Murray Balfour
Bill Hay

A20   The Chicago Cougars

A21   Socks

A22   *None Against!*

A23   Al Secord (1982–83: 58 goals)

A24   Football (The Blackhawks called him up to the team shortly after the offer was made.)

A25   Frank Mahovlich (The Big M scored 36 points to Hull's 47.)

*** HAWK FAST FACTS ***

Chicago Stadium was the site of the first Sunday afternoon game ever played in the NHL. Perhaps it was too much excitement for the Hawks: They fell to the Leafs, 3–1, in the January 20, 1952, showdown.

Q9 (Glory Days). When Pittsburgh won the 1991 Stanley Cup, it was only the second time in NHL history that a U.S. born coach led his team to the championship. This American was the first to do so. Name him.

CHICAGO BLACKHAWKS

Q10 (The Uniforms). No sibling rivalry was in evidence on the 1942-43 Blackhawks when three brothers played for Chicago, and even skated on the same line for a short time. Identify the trio.

Q40 (The Uniforms). Identify the Hawk who was suspended for 20 games after he deliberately tripped a linesman.

Q26 Bobby Hull was in good company in 1962 when he became the third player to net 50 goals in a season. What players preceded him in reaching this plateau?

Q27 With what NHL club did Hull end his playing career in 1980?

Q28 Why did Bobby Hull remove all his trophies and pucks from the Hockey Hall of Fame in 1982?

Q29 Who was given uniform No. 9 when the Golden Jet departed Chicago?

Q30 The Hawks retired Bobby Hull's No. 9. What other club honored Hull by hanging his jersey from the rafters?

Q31 What is Pit Martin's given name?

Q32 By what nickname was Stan Mikita known?

Q33 What piece of equipment did Hawk Hall of Famer Stan Mikita design in 1973?

Q34 Identify the 1992 hit movie in which Stan Mikita appeared as the owner of a doughnut shop in Aurora.

Q35 What team drafted Dirk Graham in the fifth round of the 1979 draft?

Q36 For what NFL team did Mike O'Connell's father, Tommy, play quarterback?

Q37 Drafted by the Blackhawks in the 11th round of the 1978 draft, Darryl Sutter opted to play the 1978–79 season in another country, where he was named the top rookie. In what part of the world did Sutter make his successful debut?

Q38 Darryl Sutter spent eight years in a Hawk uniform and still holds a pair of team playoff marks. What are the records?

Q39 What league award did Steve Larmer capture in 1982–83?

Q40 Identify the Hawk who was suspended for 20 games for deliberately tripping a linesman.

Q41 The 1984 Canada Cup MVP, this onetime Hawk has an ice rink named after him in his hometown of Milton, Ontario. Who was so honored?

Q42 Name the five goalies who guarded the Hawk web during the 1988–89 season.

CHICAGO BLACKHAWKS

A26 Maurice Richard
Bernie Geoffrion

A27 The Hartford Whalers (In 1981, Hull played in five exhibition games for the Rangers, but the club decided against acquiring his rights from Hartford.)

A28 Hull took back all of his memorabilia because he was against the Hall's new policy of charging admission.

A29 Dale Tallon

A30 The Winnipeg Jets

A31 Hubert Jacques

A32 "The Chippy Czech"

A33 A helmet

A34 *Wayne's World*

A35 The Vancouver Canucks

A36 The Cleveland Browns

A37 Japan

A38 Most goals in one playoff year (12)
Most overtime goals in one playoff series (2)

A39 He was named Rookie of the Year.

A40 Tom Lysiak (1983–84)

A41 John Tonelli

A42 Ed Belfour
Darren Pang
Jim Waite
Chris Clifford
Alain Chevrier

THE UNIFORMS

Q43 Greg Millen led the NHL in shutouts with six during the 1988–89 season. With what team was the veteran netminder playing?

Q44 At what Boston-area academy did Jeremy Roenick lead his team to two New England prep school titles?

Q45 The owner of the Junior A team in Hull personally recruited Jeremy Roenick to play for his team in 1988–89. What hockey great sought J.R.'s services for his Quebec club?

Q46 A Czechoslovakian native, this defenseman played for Vancouver, Toronto, and Ambri Piotta of the Swiss League before joining the Blackhawks as a free agent in September 1990. Who is he?

Q47 Ed Balfour bagged a daily double at the end of the 1990–91 season. He earned the Vezina Trophy as the top goalie and the Calder Trophy as the best rookie. What Hawk won the Selke Trophy as the NHL's best defensive forward?

Q48 Ed Belfour had a stellar 1990–91 season as he led the NHL in three of the four major goaltending categories: goals against average (2.47), wins (43), and save percentage (.910). Who edged out Belfour for most shutouts?

Q49 True or false: Steve Larmer has played in more consecutive games than any other active player in the league.

Q50 For what three NHL teams did John Tonelli play before he joined the Hawks as a free agent in the summer of 1991?

Q51 In a January 26, 1991, game against Toronto, Doug Wilson notched his first career hat trick and became only the second Chicago blueliner to score three goals in a single game. What other Hawk defenseman netted a hat trick?

Q52 Who was immediately given Doug Wilson's No. 24 when the defenseman was shipped off to the San Jose Sharks?

Q53 In the 1991–92 season, Michel Goulet became the 17th player to score 500 NHL goals. For what World Hockey Association team did Goulet net 28 goals?

CHICAGO BLACKHAWKS

A43 St. Louis Blues

A44 Thayer Academy (in Braintree, Massachusetts)

A45 Wayne Gretzky (In 28 games, Roenick had 34 goals and 36 assists.)

A46 Rick Lanz

A47 Dirk Graham

A48 Don Beaupre of the Caps had five shutouts; Belfour had four.

A49 True (As of 1991, Larmer hasn't missed a game since the 1982–83 season.)

A50 The New York Islanders (1978–86)
The Calgary Flames (1986–88)
The Los Angeles Kings (1988–91)

A51 Dick Redmond (December 12, 1977, vs. the Colorado Rockies)

A52 Kerry Toporowski (the player acquired by Chicago in the 1991 trade)

A53 Birmingham

——————————— · ———————————

*** HAWK FAST FACTS ***

ESPO EXCELLENCE
Minutes Played by a Rookie Netminder—3,763; 1969-70
Shutouts in a Season—15; 1969-70
Most Games—1,548 (including playoffs; tied)
Shutouts in a Career—74 (16 Seasons)
Consecutive Wins—8; 1980-81

*** HAWK FAST FACTS ***

MOST GOALS IN A PERIOD BY ONE PLAYER
Four—Max Bentley vs. Rangers; 1/28/43 (3rd)
Clint Smith vs. Montreal; 3/4/45 (3rd)
Grant Mulvey vs. St. Louis; 2/3/82 (1st)
Al Record vs. Toronto; 1/7/87 (2nd)

SETTING THE STANDARD

Q1 What Hawk posted the three fastest consecutive goals by a single player on March 23, 1952, against the New York Rangers?

Q2 How many whitewashes did Tony Esposito have when he set a team record for most shutouts in a season (1969–70)?

Q3 Goalies Mike Liut and Gary Edwards were bombarded in a February 1982 game as this Hawk set a team record by netting five goals in a single game. Name the sharpshooter who led the team to a 9–5 win over St. Louis.

Q4 Name the Chicago goalie who racked up the most penalty minutes in a season.

Q5 What Blackhawk holds the record for most penalty minutes in a season?

Q6 What Blackhawk set a franchise playoff record when he scored four goals in a postseason contest?

Q7 Whose team consecutive-game record did Steve Larmer shatter?

Q8 In spite of playing in only 45 games in the 1987–88 season, this goalkeep holds the club record for most assists by a netminder in a single season. Name him.

Q9 Ed Belfour set a club record in the 1990–91 season when he appeared in 72 games. How many of those contests did the Eagle start?

Q10 The 1990–91 regular season was a vintage one for the Hawks as they led the league in points—106—and matched a team record for wins in a season. How many victories did they chalk up?

Q11 What player is the club's all-time leading scorer as a defenseman in goals and points?

Q12 Michel Goulet joined an elite group of Chicago players when he notched his 500th goal as a Blackhawk. Identify the other Hawks who tallied their 500th while playing for Chicago.

Q13 Jerry Roenick bested Bobby Hull's 1962 record for most goals in a season (including playoffs). By how many goals did J.R. beat the Golden Jet's standard?

CHICAGO BLACKHAWKS

A1   Bill Mosienko (21 seconds)

A2   15

A3   Grant Mulvey (His two assists also set a club mark for most points in a game—seven.)

A4   Bob Sauve (27 minutes 1985–86)

A5   Mike Peluso (Peluso's 1991–92 season total surpassed Dave Manson's 1988–89 former record of 352 penalty minutes.)

A6   Denis Savard (April 10, 1986: 6–4 loss to Toronto)

A7   John Marks's (who played in 509 straight contests from October 27, 1973, to January 2, 1980)

A8   Darren Pang (six)

A9   68

A10   49

A11   Doug Wilson (225 goals, 779 points)

A12   Bobby Hull
Stan Mikita

A13   Four goals (Roenick had 62 goals in 1991-92.)

--- · ---

*** HAWK FAST FACTS ***

DOUG WILSON'S BLACKHAWK HIGHLIGHTS
  Club Records for:
    Highest career scoring for a defenseman—goals (225), assists (554), and points (779)
    Highest single-season scoring, defenseman—goals (39), assists (54), and total points (93)
    Shots on goal in one game—12 (11/6/83: vs. New Jersey; tied)
  Played in six All-Star Games
  Norris Trophy (NHL's top defenseman) winner (1982)

FYI

Q1 How did the Blackhawks acquire their nickname?

Q2 When the Blackhawks took to the ice for the first time (1926), the league was split into two divisions. Identify the divisions and the section to which the Hawks were assigned.

Q3 The Hawks found a new home when Chicago Stadium opened its doors in 1929. For what purpose was the $7 million sports palace originally built?

Q4 What do the Blackhawks of 1938 have in common with the 1949 edition of the Toronto Maple Leafs?

Q5 On February 20, 1944, the Blackhawks skated to a 0–0 deadlock, and neither Chicago nor its opponent was assessed a single penalty. Who did the Hawks host in that unusual contest?

Q6 On January 5, 1957, the Hawks played in the first game ever shown on network television. Who did they face off against in the historic contest?

Q7 Besides the 1990–91 season, how many times have the Blackhawks clinched first place overall in the NHL?

Q8 What actor was named the Hawks' honorary captain for the 1991–92 season?

Q9 In 1991, the Hawks hired a female figure-skating dancer to improve this player's stride and balance. Who required the tutoring?

Q10 The NHL turned back the clock at the beginning of the 1991–92 season when the league's original six teams played one another on opening night. Who did the Blackhawks face off against in the October 3rd game?

Q11 In the question above, what was unusual about the uniforms worn by the Hawks and the other five original clubs?

GLORY DAYS

Q1 In preparation for their 1939–40 first-round meeting with the Toronto Maple Leafs, the Hawks utilized a form of travel that had never been attempted by a pro team before. How did the Hawks journey to the Canadian city?

CHICAGO BLACKHAWKS

A1 The name was adopted in honor of the Blackhawk Field Gun Battalion, a unit that owner Major McLaughlin commanded in World War I.

A2 The Canadian and American divisions. Because of strict geographic guidelines, the Hawks were placed in the American Division.

A3 It was initially built as a boxing arena.

A4 They are the only teams with regular-season losing records to have won the Stanley Cup.

A5 The Toronto Maple Leafs

A6 The New York Rangers (New York thumped the Hawks, 4–1.)

A7 Twice (1966–67 and 1969–70)

A8 Jim Belushi

A9 Kerry Toporowski

A10 The Detroit Red Wings (New York played Boston, and Toronto met Montreal.)

A11 The teams were outfitted in jerseys that were replicas of their early-day uniforms.

———————————— · ————————————

A1 They flew in a chartered plane. (The Hawks had not notified Canadian officials and were delayed before they could be cleared.)

*** HAWK FAST FACTS ***

The last time a Stanley Cup Final was played in the month of April was Game 1 of the final series between the Blackhawks and the Canadiens on April 29, 1973. Montreal won, 8–3, on its home ice.

Q2 In what category did Stan Mikita lead all players in the Blackhawks' victorious Stanley Cup Championship Series?

Q3 Name the Hawk who set a Championship Series record by registering eight assists by a defenseman in 1973.

Q4 With NHL President John Ziegler unavailable, Hawk owner Bill Wirtz was forced to make a decision about the on-ice officials in a 1988 playoff game between New Jersey and Boston. What controversial call did Wirtz make?

Q5 The Blackhawks had an impressive 1990–91 regular season as they racked up a league-leading 106 points, but they could not duplicate that success in the playoffs. In a huge upset, the North Stars eliminated Chicago 4–2, and the Hawks joined one other team as the only No. 1 clubs since the 1967 league expansion to lose in the first round. With what team do the Hawks share that dubious distinction?

Q6 Who scored the North Stars' winning goal in overtime of Game 1 in the first round of the 1991 playoffs?

Q7 That overtime goal was scored on a power play. Name the Blackhawk who was assessed a four-minute penalty for high sticking at 3:40 of OT.

Q8 The feud between Doug Wilson and coach Mike Keenan intensified during the 1991 playoffs when Keenan left the ailing defenseman in Chicago as the team traveled to Minnesota for Game 6. What did Wilson do in response to the snub?

Q9 When Pittsburgh won the 1991 Stanley Cup, it was only the second time in NHL history that an American-born coach led his team to the championship. Who was the first American to do so?

Q10 After thumping St. Louis in the opening round of the 1992 playoffs, the Hawks swept Detroit in four games in the Norris Division Finals. Prior to the Red Wing victory, when was the last time Chicago completed a sweep in a best-of-seven series?

Q11 The Hawks established an NHL record during the 1992 playoffs when they won 11 consecutive postseason games. Whose record did Chicago surpass?

Q12 In the first game of Chicago's 1992 playoff match with Edmonton, the Hawks scored the fastest three goals in their playoff history. What players combined to net the goals?

CHICAGO BLACKHAWKS

A2 Scoring

A3 Pat Stapleton (The mark was matched by Edmonton's Paul Coffey in 1985 and surpassed in 1991 by Pittsburgh's Larry Murphy.)

A4 Wirtz decided that amateur officials could work the game after the regulars walked off the job in a last-minute dispute with the league.

A5 The Boston Bruins (who lost to Montreal in 1971)

A6 Brian Propp

A7 Keith Brown

A8 Wilson bought his own ticket and flew to Minneapolis so he could attend the game.

A9 Chicago's Bill Stewart (1938)

A10 1978 (against Philadelphia)

A11 The Boston Bruins (1970: 10 games)

A12 Mike Peluso (2:51 of the second period)
Jeremy Roenick (3:20)
Steve Smith (4:17)
(Total time: 1 minute, 26 seconds)

*** HAWK FAST FACTS ***

NO PLACE LIKE HOME?
   The Hawks own the NHL record for the fewest home victories in a season. They registered only two victories in the 22 games played at home during the 1927–28 season.

*** HAWK FAST FACTS ***

During the 1928–29 season, the Blackhawks were shut out in consecutive games, an NHL record. That season, they also established league marks for the longest home winless streak (15 games), fewest goals in a season (33), and lowest goals-per-game average (.75).

GLORY DAYS

Q13 The Hawks and Penguins met only once before in postseason play prior to 1992. What was the outcome of that series?

Q14 Chicago's Mike Keenan and Pittsburgh's Scotty Bowman were both previously employed by one NHL club at the same time. What organization had the two under contract?

Q15 In Game 1 of the 1992 Stanley Cup Finals, Mario Lemieux tallied the game winner on a power play with 13 seconds remaining in the third period. Who hooked Super Mario to give Pittsburgh the man advantage?

Q16 During the 1992 playoffs, Pittsburgh equaled a postseason mark established by the Hawks. What record is that?

TRADES, WAIVES, AND ACQUISITIONS

Q1 In one of the franchise's biggest trades, the Hawks sent their star center to Toronto in exchange for five players: Bob Goldham, Bud Poile, Gaye Stewart, Gus Bodnar, and Ernie Dickens. Who went north of the border in the 1947 deal?

Q2 Prior to the 1951–52 season, the Hawks purchased six players from the Red Wings. It was the biggest cash deal in NHL history at that time. How much did the team shell out?

Q3 In a 1957 swap with Toronto, the Hawks traded Forbes Kennedy and John Wilson to the Leafs. What combo came to Chicagoland in return?

Q4 Reg Fleming, Ab McDonald, and Murray Balfour were shipped to Boston in a 1964 swap with the Bean Towners. What player came to the Blackhawks in return?

Q5 In a deal that was considered a steal for Chicago, the Hawks dispatched John McKenzie to Boston for a young blueliner who became a stalwart on the team. Identify the player involved in the 1965 trade.

Q6 The Hawks were wheeling and dealing with the Rangers in early 1965 when the two teams engineered a six-player deal. The Hawks shipped Doug Robinson, John Brenneman, and Wayne Hillman to New York in exchange for Don Johns, Bill Taylor, and this Ranger captain. Who was he?

CHICAGO BLACKHAWKS

A13   Chicago swept Pittsburgh four straight games in the 1972 quarterfinal matchup.

A14   The Buffalo Sabres (While Bowman was coach and general manager of the Adams Division club, Keenan coached the Sabres' farm club in Rochester, New York.)

A15   Steve Smith

A16   Consecutive postseason victories (By sweeping Chicago, the Penguins tied the 11-game mark that the Hawks had established during the 1992 playoffs. Ironically, it was Pittsburgh that ended the Hawks' streak while setting their own.)

A1   Doug Bentley (The Hawks also included Cy Thomas in the swap.)

A2 $75,000 (The Hawks acquired Clare Raglan, Max McNab, George Gee, Jim McFadden, Jim Peters, and Clare Martin.)

A3   Ted Lindsay
Glenn Hall

A4   Doug Mohns

A5   Pat "Whitey" Stapleton

A6   Camille Henry

*** HAWK FAST FACTS ***

Ed Olczyk was the first American-born player selected No. 1 in the draft (1984) by his hometown team.

*** HAWK FAST FACTS ***

The Stadium has the only main press box in the NHL that is suspended at the end of the rink.

TRADES, WAIVES, AND ACQUISITIONS

Q7 The Blackhawks sent Jerry Korab and Gary Smith to Vancouver in a 1973 transaction with the Canucks. What player came to the Second City in return?

Q8 In 1974, Tommy Ivan engineered an even-up deal with California when he dealt Len Frig to the Seals. What centerman came to Chicagoland in the trade?

Q9 Who was the first player drafted by Bob Pulford after he became the Hawks' GM in 1977?

Q10 In one of the biggest deals in years, the Hawks traded Ivan Boldirev, Darcy Rota, and Phil Russell for Greg Fox, Tom Lysiak, Pat Ribble, Miles Zaharko, and Harold Philipoff. To what now-defunct franchise did the three Hawks go in the 1979 swap?

Q11 What defenseman was traded to the Bruins in exchange for Al Secord in a 1980 swap?

Q12 The Canadiens bypassed Denis Savard as the first pick overall in the 1980 draft. Who did they select instead of the speedy center in the top spot?

Q13 Name the blueliner who came to the Hawks in a 1983 trade with the Flyers in exchange for Doug Crossman and a draft pick.

Q14 In early 1983, the Hawks traded Tony Tanti to the Vancouver Canucks. What American-born forward came to Chicago in return?

Q15 In 1984, Bob Pulford traded Chicago native Bob Janecyk to the Los Angeles Kings so that the Hawks would be able to draft another local product. Who is this Windy City native?

Q16 Who shuffled off to Buffalo when the Blackhawks acquired Adam Creighton in a 1988 deal with the Sabres?

Q17 After four seasons in an Islander uniform, this blueliner came to Chicagoland in exchange for Gary Nylund and Marc Bergevin in late 1988. Name him.

Q18 Name the pair of Nordiques who came to the Hawks in a 1990 deal for Everett Sanipass, Dan Vincelette, and Mario Doyon.

Q19 On the day of the 1990–91 trading deadline, the Hawks reacquired Dan Vincelette along with forward Paul Gillis from the Quebec Nordiques. Who did they give up in the transaction?

CHICAGO BLACKHAWKS

A7   Dale Tallon

A8   Ivan Boldirev

A9   Doug Wilson

A10   The Atlanta Flames

A11   Mike O'Connell

A12   Doug Wickenheiser

A13   Behn Wilson

A14   Curt Fraser

A15   Ed Olczyk

A16   Rick Vaive

A17   Steve Konroyd

A18   Michel Goulet
      Greg Millen

A19   Minor leaguers Ryan McGill and Mike McNeil

*** HAWK FAST FACTS ***

TOP SCORERS—1926–1992

——— Goals ———		——— Assists ———	
Bobby Hull	604	Stan Mikita	926
Stan Mikita	541	Denis Savard	662
Denis Savard	351	Bobby Hull	549
Steve Larmer	298	Doug Wilson	525
Dennis Hull	298	Pierre Pilote	400

*** HAWK FAST FACTS ***

On January 12, 1986, Denis Savard scored four seconds into the third period in a game against the Hartford Whalers. This equaled the NHL mark for the fastest goal at the start of a period, which was set by Claude Provost of the Montreal Canadiens (11/9/57).

TRADES, WAIVES, AND ACQUISITIONS

Q20 The Hawks traded goalie Jacques Cloutier to the Quebec Nordiques in early 1991 for veteran winger Tony McKegney. What team selected McKegney in the second round of the 1978 amateur draft?

Q21 In a midsummer 1991 trade, the Hawks dealt Selke Trophy winner Troy Murray and Warren Rychel to the Jets. What twosome came to Chicagoland in the swap with Winnipeg?

Q22 In September 1991, the Hawks traded Doug Wilson to the San Jose Sharks for a draft choice and a 20-year-old minor leaguer. Name the young prospect.

Q23 It was a D-day deal on October 2, 1991, when Steve Smith came to the Hawks for a defenseman who had been Chicago's first-round pick in 1985. What blueliner went to Edmonton in the deal?

Q24 Name the tandem traded to the Islanders in return for Brent Sutter and Brad Lauer in an October 1991 swap with New York.

Q25 Who did the Hawks deal to Calgary in return for Stephane Matteau in a December 1991 trade?

Q26 Identify the blueliner who was shipped to Hartford in January 1992 in exchange for Rob Brown.

Q27 What veteran did the Hawks deal to Quebec in return for Jeff Jackson in a February 1992 trade?

CHICAGO BLACKHAWKS

A20 The Buffalo Sabres (McKegney played for Buffalo, Quebec, Minnesota, the Rangers, St. Louis, Detroit, and Quebec—again.)

A21 Bryan Marchment
Chris Norton

A22 Kerry Toporowski

A23 Dave Manson

A24 Steve Thomas
Adam Creighton

A25 Trent Yawney

A26 Steve Konroyd

A27 John Tonelli

*** HAWK FAST FACTS ***

Stan Mikita was the first player in NHL history to win the Ross, Hart, and Lady Byng trophies in the same season. He did it twice: 1966–67 and 1967–68.

*** HAWK FAST FACTS ***

STAN MIKITA—"MOSTS" FOR THE BLACKHAWKS
   Most Seasons—21
   Most Games—1,548 (including playoffs; tied)
   Most Playoff Games—155
   Most 20-or-More-Goal Seasons—14
   Most Consecutive 20-or-More-Goal Seasons—14 (1961 62 to
      1974 75)
   Most Career Playoff Points—150
   Most Consecutive Games with Assists—14